"Humility, gratitude, grace, and faith Bethel Grove takes modesty 'Beyond Your Wardrobe.' I love that she dives right in by going to the heart of the issue, but she isn't afraid to answer the questions we all know every girl has, and still brings it back to what's in our hearts in the end. Reading Bethel's book is like talking to a big sister. She isn't afraid to share her opinion, but you know she is pointing you in the right direction."

Heather Hart – Director of FindingYourTrueBeauty.com

"Bethel is a rising voice out of the young generation on behalf of modesty. She speaks out of her own experience, vulnerability, passion, and research. It is refreshing to find someone in your corner who, 'gets it' when it comes to the tensions of this topic. But more importantly, she dives deeper past the rules and into the heart."

Danielle Brown – Kids Lead Pastor of 7 years

"*Beyond Your Wardrobe* takes a deeper look into modesty while reminding the reader of their tremendous value in Christ. God's word is clear and speaks to modesty for both young men and young women and shows its direct correlation with the condition of the heart. Challenging and thought-provoking you will appreciate this exploration of the idea of modesty."

Jeff Dungan – Father of a Princess Worth Dying For

"*Beyond Your Wardrobe* is an incredible read full of the truth about God's opinion when it comes to modesty compared to the opinions of society. Reading the book I actually felt that it further opened my eyes to everything I was taught by Bethel in her bible study...I highly recommend it to women of all ages struggling to define God's opinions when it comes to modesty."

Katie M – High School Senior

"Bethel Grove's *Beyond Your Wardrobe* is thought-provoking and challenging, in a good way! What a wonderful book. It is a timely reminder for some of us, and a straightforward introduction for others. Modesty is a lost art and an overlooked concern for many men and women of faith. As she says, we need to honor God with our bodies.

She reminds us to have the right mindset for all of our decisions, not just our attire. This book will make you consider your choices and your motivations behind them. God bless Bethel for using Scripture to be her guide. Let us all take note."

Karen Parkison – Teacher, Mother, and Youth Leader

"Bethel has some insights about modesty that were new to me. Having read and thought a lot about modesty, I was pleased to still be learning from Bethel's writing. It is refreshing to see a woman living out modesty and practicing what she teaches."

Dessa C – Wife and Mother of 6

"If you're like most men, you probably have no idea what a big deal this issue is for women. Reading this book will help you understand the challenges that women face today in making wise and godly decisions regarding their clothing, and you'll be better equipped to support the women in your life in their wardrobe choices. Plus, there's also some great advice for men when it comes to their clothing choices as seen through the eyes of our sisters in Christ."

Matt Stafford – College Professor

"This book is an excellent source for the truth about modesty, and not just for young teen girls and young adult women, but for anyone who might not fully understand what the Scriptures have to say about it. The author truly believes this and writes it in a way that is relatable and easily understandable."

Cody Lynn - Older Sister and Daughter

"In this book, Bethel talks about a topic that has been misrepresented by society. As you dive into this book, it becomes clear that modesty is about representing Jesus, and representing yourself as God's masterpiece."

Madeline Dungan – Mixed Media Artist

Beyond Your Wardrobe

Beyond Your Wardrobe

Finding Freedom in Embracing God's Call to Modesty and Unfading Beauty

Beyond Your Wardrobe: Finding Freedom in Embracing God's Call to Modesty and Unfading Beauty

To "My Girls": Katie, Jaylee, Maddy D, Savannah, Emma, Abby, Maddie E, Rachelle, and Samantha. This book and the lessons it teaches would not have happened without each one of you. I pray that you always believe that you are a princess worth dying for.

Contents

Introduction –
Why We Just Don't Get It

We all know people who just don't get it. The person who laughs five minutes after someone tells them a joke. The student that just doesn't understand what the teacher is telling him. We've all known people like them or perhaps have even been that person a few more times than we want to admit. But what's worse is when someone continues to repeat the same mistakes over and over, never really learning from the consequences of their previous choices. Maybe you've known someone that is heading into a physically or emotionally dangerous situation, but you cannot convince them to walk away. This type of situation can be a powerful reminder that if we don't learn from the past, we are likely to repeat our mistakes. I will use a popular movie to illustrate.

When Disney's *Frozen* was released in November 2013, it took the world by storm. I remember how shocked I was to see it become so popular so quickly, but I came to enjoy it as I watched my oldest nephew love that movie from the first time he saw it. However, one of the biggest gaps in the plot from my perspective is that there are a few characters that just don't get it. It's not Anna, Kristof, Sven, or even Olaf that can't put the pieces together; it's King Agnarr, Queen Iduna, and Elsa. This point was illustrated well with the YouTube video, "How Frozen Should Have Ended."[1] [Video link available in the back of the book]

Despite their best intentions, the king and queen didn't recognize that fear was her enemy and love was the solution. By teaching Elsa "conceal, don't feel," her parents unknowingly taught her to suppress the one emotion she needed to feel to control her powers - love. While I get why Grand Pabbie didn't just come out and say, "The answer is love," Elsa had plenty of opportunities to find this solution sooner if she had just listened to Anna. At one point, Elsa asked Anna what power her sister had to stop her, convinced no one could. However, the truth was that Anna was one of the only people who could help Elsa because Anna was the person she loved the most. By the end of the film, when Elsa hears that love will thaw, she finally gets it, but it's interesting to think about how different the story would have turned out if she had just listened to Anna.

The same thing happens within the church. Many of us hear the truth of God's Word over and over again, but we never let it sink in. We often take it at its surface value but never take the opportunity to learn the heart of the truths within it so we can apply it to our lives. Instead, we try to do things our own way. I think that this is especially true when it comes to modesty. When this topic is discussed, many of us tend to act like Elsa's parents or Elsa herself. Like Elsa's parents, some try to address the physical symptoms of immodesty by making rules to keep everyone in line, all the while ignoring the underlying condition that's causing the problem: the attitude of our heart. Others choose to respond like Elsa, just throwing out the rules and living the way they want. Both of these responses often cause hurt and emotional pain, either to ourselves or those we love.

Our tendencies to respond this way are a result of the lies that our culture constantly feeds us about our worth and identity. They cause our hearts to be enslaved by the false ideals we've accepted as the truth, and this results in a fundamental gap in our understanding of our value, which impacts our ability to embrace biblical modesty. In situations like these, the world tries to convince us that living according to God's Word will inhibit us from living our lives to the fullest. However, through my study and research, I have found that God's Word is the very place where freedom can be discovered by anyone who chooses to embrace it. This is especially true when it comes to modesty. We do not usually associate the words "modesty" and "freedom" with one another, but I pray that you will by the end of this book. Because when I began to embrace the call to modesty in my own life, it came to change the way I saw myself and the way I saw everyone around me.

This book is written for those who want to go deeper. I hope girls and women of all ages will be a part of this journey. I even hope that some men will be willing to join us to gain a biblical perspective on this topic. This journey won't be an easy one. It may be uncomfortable as you have to rewire your mindset to see things from God's perspective instead of a worldly viewpoint. I believe the rewards will be worth the work and will help you live your life in the freedom of God's grace, not a bunch of manmade rules. I am hoping that you will join me so that we can experience this freedom together. Let's get started.

PART 1

Discerning the Lies

1. Lies We Believe about Physical Beauty

While I was a student at a Christian college, I was blessed to have the opportunity to spend a week in New York City for a seminar class. That trip was an experience I will never forget. I had never been to New York, and it was only the second time in my life that I traveled by airplane. This class, called "Exegeting the City," helped us learn how to make Christianity work in an urban context. I learned so much on that trip, but there is one experience that stands out from the others because it taught me a lot about how the world perceives fashion and beauty.

During our first lecture, our professor explained to us that rich people are just people like you and me, even if there is a cultural gap between us. To help us bridge this gap, we were given a special assignment. Together, we walked to one of the fanciest and most expensive retail stores in the United States, Bergdorf Goodman. We were given instructions to go into the store, find the formal clothing department, and try those clothes on, regardless of the price tag. The men went to the men's store across the street and the ladies went into the women's store. Even before we got to the formal wear department, we all felt like a fish out of water. When we finally found the formal gowns, it was like we were on a completely different planet. We looked through the dresses together, but most of us were scared about trying them on since we would have to ask the attendants. I was quite nervous myself, but I had been preparing myself since a friend told me about the assignment before the trip. So I was the brave one that asked first. I will never forget the contrast in the attendants' reactions. The first one was polite and helpful, as would be expected. She even informed me that the dress was available in other colors. The other one gave me a glance that said, "You don't have enough money to be touching that dress. You don't belong here." I guess my clothes had given away that I was not part of the top 1% clientele that they usually served, but her glance of judgment based on what I was wearing is something I have never forgotten.

The nice attendant helped me to my fitting room and eventually, the other girls worked up the courage to ask as well. The fitting room was the size of my current bedroom. (Ok, maybe not, but it was still huge). It even had one of those round modeling podiums. The dress I picked was a silver strapless mermaid with layered fabric. Although it was pretty, it almost seemed like the kind of dress I could find in the prom section of a local department store. I'm sure the materials were of superior quality, but it didn't seem like the kind of dress I would search for in a store like this. I took some pictures and took the dress off. Up to this point, I don't think I had taken notice of the price, so I finally looked at the price tag: $4,330. I remember thinking to myself: *who in their right mind would pay this much for a dress like this?* Part of me started to think that the rude attendant had a point.

ADDRESSING THE LIES

Many of us believe things that just aren't true, whether we realize it or not. I believe the rude sales attendant had bought into the many of the lies that had been sold to her about a woman's value. Our culture sells these lies using many different mediums: TV, movies, books, magazines, social media, and the list could go on.[1] They use these mediums to try and convince us that we can find our

18

happiness through worldly means, such as achieving popularity, receiving praise for our beauty, or having a successful career. Buying into these lies will cause us to live our lives apart from what God has in store for us, and will make it harder to live our lives in light of the truth.

As I've sort to better understand what we are up against, I've come to believe that some of the most difficult lies that women face today involve their self-worth and physical appearance. Many of us spend our time chasing beauty standards that are impossible to obtain and therefore, we are never satisfied. This is why we have to take the time to discern the truth and remove the lies we've believed from our mindset. After all, if we don't learn how to have our identity firmly rooted in Christ and His truth, we will never discover the heart motivation we need for living a modest life. So we are going to begin this journey by walking through several different lies that many of us believe about our physical appearance, so we can learn to see ourselves as God sees us instead of how the world sees us. Let's take a look:

1. Our Worth Is Tied To Our Physical Beauty

Although this is something that most of us would never say outright, many of us find ourselves caught in the cycle of believing that the gorgeous models and celebrities we see on TV are worth more because everyone sees them as beautiful. Whether they realize it or not, Hollywood continually communicates that their beauty is connected to their happiness and success. This often leads the women watching to think "If I had what she has, then I would be happy," or "If I was as beautiful as her, then I would have worth."

19

Even young girls are starting to believe these lies. When authors Dannah Gresh and Nancy DeMoss Wolgemuth surveyed over 1,500 Christian girls ages 7-12, they found that almost half of them were unhappy with their outward appearance.[2] If this is the way elementary and early junior high age girls feel, despite having faith in Jesus, it's hard to imagine how much more insecurity they would carry with them into their teen years and adulthood if they continue to listen to the world without filtering its messages through God's Word.

While it's true that our world tends to put more value on movie stars and models because of their beauty, wealth, and success, the stars and models themselves have the same struggles as many average women when it comes to maintaining their beauty and social status. This is because they buy into the same lies that we do about our worth and identity.[3] They long to be valued and respected, but haven't realized that the methods they use to find their worth aren't working. If you take some time to look up the life stories of actresses like Marilyn Monroe and Judy Garland, you will quickly find that their personal lives were quite miserable, despite the beauty and fame they acquired. Their "success" stories will not lead to your happiness, no matter what Hollywood tries to tell you.

The truth of the matter is that your worth is not dependent on the opinions of others. This is good news for us because opinions are subject to change. Not to mention that our society's standards for beauty are constantly changing. Your worth will never be defined by anything you can do to yourself or for yourself. Your worth was defined the moment that you were first conceived in your mother's womb.

"For you formed my inward parts; you knitted me together in my mother's womb. I praise you, for I am fearfully and wonderfully made. Wonderful are your works; my soul knows it very well. My frame was not hidden from you, when I was being made in secret, intricately woven in the depths of the earth. Your eyes saw my unformed substance; in your book were written, every one of them, the days that were formed for me, when as yet there was none of them." (Psalm 139:13-16 ESV)

If we have our hope rooted firmly in Jesus Christ, we know that we are made fearfully and wonderfully *imago dei* (a Latin phrase that means "in the image of God"). I encourage you to take a minute to let that truth sink in. You were uniquely made, down to your very last cell, by the Creator of the universe. He knows the days of your life and takes joy in seeing the days of your life unfold. No matter if there are features you have that you dislike or anyone tries to demean, you can hold onto the knowledge that you are a masterpiece created by God. There is no one exactly like you. This means that you have a purpose for your life that goes far beyond your wardrobe or your physical appearance. This gives me hope on days when I don't like what I see in the mirror. I hope it does for you too, and that this purpose will become clear to you as we continue through this book.

2. It's the Guy's Fault if He's Tempted

There is a scene that I frequently see in TV shows and movies that drives me crazy every time I see it: A female character is dressed sexy for a date. Then, this woman notices that her male friend is staring at her cleavage, so she instructs him not to look. This woman is upset when any other man other than her date notices what she has on display, especially if he is her friend. After all, her intention in dressing sexy was to impress her date and only her date. The other men around her should know better than to keep looking. This reminds me of a story I heard about two of my older sister's high school friends that were in a similar situation. The girl was wearing a very low-cut top at a party and continued to bend over, showing off her chest. It finally got to the point when her guy friend said to her:

Guy: Can you please quit bending over?
Girl: Why don't you quit looking?!
Guy: Well, I am a guy.

What all of these women, and many others like them, fail to realize is that you cannot pick and choose who notices your body if you are exposed in public. It bothers me that so many women are convinced that they can control the attention they attract when they expose themselves. In truth, the only way to control that is to only expose yourself in the context of marriage, where only your husband sees. That's the way it was designed to work. If you are aware that men are visually charged and you still choose to expose yourself, then you are responsible for putting the temptation you put in front of them.

Have you ever heard of the Gestalt theory? If you haven't, let me try to summarize one of its main concepts: if we see an incomplete picture, we crave for its completion. [4] For example, if you look at an abstract piece of artwork, you usually try to find some familiar concept in the picture to complete it in your mind. This is not just true of paintings. When we see someone dressed immodestly, there is a tendency to fill in the missing parts or complete the picture in our minds. It's a fact. This should make us think twice about what we wear.

As far as the guy's responsibility in this, we need to realize that temptation in and of itself is not a sin. It's the beginning of the process of how Satan leads us to sin, but it only becomes sin when you dwell and/or act on the temptation. Since God will always provide a way for us to walk away from temptation (1 Corinthians 10:13), choosing to indulge your temptation means that you have to assume responsibility for your actions. When a man sees an inappropriately dressed woman, he has not immediately sinned. He only sins if he keeps looking and thinking about her body, or if he tries to act on those thoughts.

If you are aware that Satan is the one that tempts us, then why do you want to participate in Satan's work by dressing provocatively? Do you want to play the role of Satan in someone's life? That part is your responsibility and choosing to do so willfully is a sin.

We also need to realize that sexual temptation is not just a guy problem. Women can also fall into sexual temptation when we dwell on inappropriate images in our minds. In the same way, we have to acknowledge that immodesty isn't just a girl problem. There are plenty of men who attract too much attention to their bodies with the way they dress. It's important to remember that both genders have both responsibilities, avoiding creating temptation while also avoiding falling into temptation.

3. MODESTY MEANS BEING ASHAMED OF MY BODY

Our culture continually tries to convince us that there is freedom found in dressing or acting however we want. Feminists have tried to tell us for years that if we are not for women's liberation, then we must be advocating women's oppression. So by this same line of logic, we are

23

ashamed of our bodies because we refuse to flaunt them. Bethany Beal of Girl Defined Ministries shared the story of when she interviewed at a modeling agency as a teenager but decided to pass on the opportunity because she didn't want to compromise her moral standards. The man that interviewed her, disappointed by her choice, told her that when she got older and learned how to be "comfortable in [her] own skin" that she should come back to see him.[5] Can you believe he said that? Bethany *was* comfortable in her skin. She just knew that she didn't need to strip down in front of the camera to prove it.

I've known plenty of women like Bethany that dress modestly and are appropriately confident in their bodies. These are the women who embrace that they were created *imago dei* and are aware of the power that God gave them to be physically attractive to men. Instead of using this power for selfish reasons, they choose to dress modestly to save that power for just one man. By choosing to hold back until the right time to reveal your body, you instead reveal your dignity to the world around you. It's because I'm grateful for the body that God gave me that I choose to preserve it for the right time and place to use it. Just like actress Jessica Rey said, "Modesty isn't about hiding ourselves; it's about revealing our dignity." [6]

4. I DON'T HAVE TO LISTEN TO MY PARENTS ABOUT THE CLOTHES I WEAR

Have you ever been the girl hunched over saying, "But Mom, my shirt is totally long enough"? Or have you ever felt that your parents needed to mind their own business when it comes to the clothes you wear? After all, your parents don't know what it's like to be a teenager in the 2020s. If fashion is always changing, then why should I listen to them?

If you have had these thoughts, you're not alone, but you need to realize that your parents love you and want what's best for you. The Scriptures continually call us to honor our father and our mother, even if we don't like what they have to say. Honoring our parents is one of the only commandments given in the Scriptures with a promise: "that your days may be long in the land the Lord your God has given you." (Exodus 20:12b ESV) Although this is technically meant to be a promise to the children of Israel, I almost feel like it's common sense: if you listen to the wisdom of your parents, who have probably lived 20 to 30 more years of life than you have, then you will probably live longer. You will be much less likely to do stupid things that could result in your untimely end! That's part of the reason that God designed the family unit the way He did.

If you are having trouble communicating with your parents about your fashion choices, you should find a time to sit down to talk to them. I know this isn't the most comfortable thing to do, but hopefully, you will be able to find a way to dress that honors their rules but doesn't make you feel like you're wearing a brown paper sack. Make sure to pay attention to your dad when he is concerned about your outfit choices. He is one of the best ways for you to hear the truth from a guy's perspective. It's his job to provide for and protect you. Valuing his feedback on your wardrobe will help you gain wisdom to make better choices later in your life.

5. I SHOULD BE ABLE TO DO (OR WEAR) WHATEVER I WANT WITH NO CONSEQUENCES

This lie is one that manifests itself in different ways, but is really at the heart of so much of the sin that separates us from God. In some ways, this topic is ironic, because sin is the very reason we have to wear clothes in the first place. When Adam and Eve chose to disobey God by eating the forbidden fruit in the Garden of Eden, the very first thing they became aware of was their nakedness (Genesis 3:7). Suddenly, the beauty of what God had designed was tainted by the knowledge that it was wrong for them to be publicly exposed. Their nakedness was a reminder of their sin. So when God realized that they were ashamed of their nakedness, He had compassion on them and made them clothes out of animal skins, replacing the insufficient ones they made for themselves out of figs leaves (Genesis 3:21).

Since then, humanity has been fighting a never-ending battle against the very thing that God gave us as a gift: free will. God has always wanted to give his people a choice. He never wants to force any decision on us, especially when it comes to our relationship with Him. He wants us to choose Him. It's incredible to think that God could have chosen to design all of humanity as puppets that would instantly obey his commands (like Anne Hathaway's character in the movie *Ella Enchanted*), but He chose to give us the freedom to do what we choose with the lives we've been given. When you think about it that way, it's pretty humbling.

Unfortunately, after sin entered the world, our motives were not always pure. After Adam and Eve abused the gift of free will, we no longer had our hearts centered on doing God's will, because we were aware that we have the option of doing things our way. Therefore, we can't do everything our heart desires without checking it against the truth of God's word. Paul makes this point in 1 Corinthians when he explains, "'I have the right to do anything,' you say—but not everything is beneficial." (1 Corinthians 6:12 NIV). In other words, "You keep saying, 'I can do anything I want,' but not everything you're allowed to do is helpful or wise."

Although this freedom is an incredible gift from God, we are usually left to deal with the consequences of our actions if we or someone else chooses to sin. In that way, free will is a double-edged sword. This is where this lie becomes so dangerous. The world tries to tell us that not only can we do whatever we want, but we don't have to suffer any consequences for our actions. A young woman can have sex before marriage, have an abortion after getting pregnant, and never have to deal with the consequences of her decisions. Or a teen boy can tell his parents he's no longer a Christian, move out of the house, and not have to live with the repercussions of his choices. However, there is simply no logical way for this to be a possibility. The truth of the matter is if you aren't suffering the consequences of your actions, there is usually someone else who is. Someone always has to suffer for our sins. Getting to the point where you refuse to acknowledge your sin will usually end up hurting those you love. That refusal to acknowledge your sin is a sin in and of itself.

As we talked about previously, you cannot wear whatever you want and choose who sees what you have exposed. If you put it on display for one, you put it on display for all. You are setting men up for temptation and not truly honoring the God you profess to worship. Other people will suffer because of your actions. That's the very situation we should be trying to avoid.

2. Lies We Believe about Modesty

Modesty is a word that can make some women cringe. Those that do are usually filled with dread as they think about their preconceived expectations about the way they should dress: everything from strict rules that vary between churches or institutions, to being forced to wear clothing that reminds them of what women wore a hundred years ago. By and large, this is what many people stereotype to be the essence of biblical modesty, despite this definition consisting mostly of manmade rules and personal preferences rather than Scriptural instructions.

However, when you take the time to look at many of the assumptions these people have about modesty, you very quickly realize that their version of modesty doesn't work. It doesn't match up with the literal meaning of the word or what the Bible teaches about it. So we are going to break down several lies that many people, Christians and non-Christians alike, believe about the concept of modesty. Let's take a look:

1. Modesty is a list of rules I have to follow

For many Christians that have grown up in more traditional denominations, the word "modesty" may conjure up memories of a list of rules they were asked to follow, especially when they were at church or doing youth activities. These rules looked different between different churches, but there was one rule that was pretty much universal at most camps and youth events: if a girl did not have a one-piece swimsuit, she had to wear a dark-colored t-shirt on top of her bikini. As I observed, this would tend to make the girls who wore bikinis mad every single time the issue would be brought up. The rules didn't change from year to year, but they usually refused to find a one-piece suit before the next camp season, even though they knew the rules and could have found an alternative swimsuit before the event started. Instead, these girls just learned to resent the rules, assuming that this was what modesty was all about.

Despite what many people have believed, the Bible does not give a specific list of "do's and do not's" when it comes to how we should dress. Personally, there are days that I wish that it did. It would be easier than trying to guess what is too short or too revealing. However, I think that the Lord knew that clothing would change with the culture. I also think He knew that if there were an official set of rules, we would be more likely to intentionally rebel against them or try to see how much we could get away with before crossing the line. God sent His Son to die on the cross for our sins so that we wouldn't be required to follow a bunch of rules to have a relationship with Him. That means when it comes to clothing, we have to learn how to let everyone, including ourselves, off the hook.

2. MODESTY IS ALL ABOUT THE CLOTHES I WEAR

When you mention the word "modesty" around non-Christians, they will most likely associate it with women's clothing and how much it doesn't reveal of her body. This view of modesty is only partially true. Although clothing does have a lot to do with modesty, it's not the only part of this concept we need to understand. In my mind, modesty isn't a state of dress:

Modesty is an attitude

Let me give an example: have you ever heard someone say, "Oh, he's just being modest"? They probably were not talking about his wardrobe. They were talking about his humility about his accomplishments. He had the opportunity to highlight his work, but he chose to give the credit to someone else who helped him. He decided not to draw attention to himself and instead focused it on something else. This is the way we should look at modesty. We need to learn to develop an attitude that doesn't desire to draw unnecessary attention to ourselves but instead wants to focus it on the God we worship. We will discuss what this looks like in chapters to come, but for now, we have to make sure we don't fall into the trap of assuming that modesty is only about necklines or hemlines.

3. MODESTY IS OUT OF DATE

The standards for what society deems as modest have changed a lot over the years. In some ways, changes do need to happen with the changes in culture. I am grateful to live in a day and age where I can wear jeans and t-shirts instead of always having to wear dresses or skirts. Unfortunately, many modern cultures have reached the point of deciding to disregard basic standards of public decency in the name of fashion. Now, we are encouraged by the fashion industry to expose parts of our bodies that were never meant to be publicly exposed. When someone objects, the fashion industry claims that the standards of public decency, which have existed for thousands of years, are irrelevant and need to change with the times.

This point of view isn't just a bad idea; it's a dangerous idea. We've already talked about how someone will always suffer the consequences of our actions. Taking this point of view just means that you are shifting the blame, throwing your conscience out the window, and letting other people suffer for your poor wardrobe choices. Please, take responsibility for your actions and don't fall into the trap of blaming someone else for your bad choices. This lie was, in part, born out of the assumption that the clothing that is considered modest by Christian standards is out of fashion and out of style. That brings us to the next lie.

4. BUT THEN I CAN'T WEAR CUTE CLOTHES ANYMORE!

When some women think of modesty, they start to picture women wearing out of date clothing from the late 1800s, or their great-great-grandmother sitting on the porch of a log cabin in a plain Amish style dress, knitting to comfort herself from the fact that she's an old maid. I have heard two words commonly associated with modesty, words that put this concept in a negative light: frumpy and dumpy. Aside from sounding like bad names for the seven dwarfs, this description for clothing is not appealing to anyone. Many of these young women honestly believe that they have to give up wearing anything attractive or fashionable to meet the biblical standard of modesty.

This, again, is a statement that is simply not true. Although it can be a lot harder to find clothing that is both modest and fashionable, it is not impossible. It does mean that you are less likely to be able to wear something straight off the rack. You may not be able to wear all the latest fashion trends the same way everyone else does, but you can still find stylish clothing with a little time and diligence. A lot of the time, it just takes wearing an extra layer or two to make an immodest outfit into one that is both modest and fashionable. All you have to do is put effort into looking in the right places. (We will discuss modesty tips and ideas in later chapters, so stay tuned.)

5. MODESTY AND SEXUAL PURITY ARE NOT RELATED

Although this book is not about sexual purity specifically, it's important to acknowledge that these topics do go hand-in-hand. One of my favorite authors of all time is Dannah Gresh. Her book, *The Secret Keeper: The Delicate Power of Modesty*, is the book that began to help me develop a passion for this topic, even while I was still in high school. However, Dannah didn't get her start in writing books about modesty. Many of her books up to the early 2000s were about sexual purity. Around that time, she felt the Lord was convicting her that she needed to teach modesty, which also meant that she would need to practice modesty herself. She resisted and didn't want to give up some of her clothes, but she came to realize how much the subjects of purity and modesty are related to each other.[1] In the end, she knew she had to make some changes to fulfill God's call, and so she did.

Several years later, she not only wrote *The Secret Keeper* and its devotional guide, but she eventually founded a ministry geared toward pre-teens to address this topic. True Girl, originally called Secret Keeper Girl, teaches tween girls about modesty and self-worth at an age-appropriate level with an interactive yearly stage tour for moms and their daughters. She's written many, many books for that age group, even more than she did for older teen girls. It became bigger than Dannah could have possibly imagined. All because she took up the call to start recognizing modesty as part of a life of purity.

I think it's easier to remember that modesty and purity are related if you're focusing on modesty. It's more of a struggle for those focused on being "technically pure", but are ignoring all the other parts of the holiness that God calls us to live a sexually pure life. Modesty is a huge part of that, especially when you realize that modesty begins with your attitude. I think our perspective on both topics would be radically different if we began to look at it this way.

6. IF THE BIBLE DOESN'T TELL ME I CAN WEAR IT, THEN I CAN'T WEAR IT AT ALL

Although this is not a lie that our society believes as a whole, this is a lie that has been bought by some Christian denominations that embrace more conservative traditions. Accepting this line of logic limits our ability to experience the freedom we have in Christ. Let me give an example that doesn't involve clothes. There is one group of churches that stands out because of their stance on worship music. When studying the Scriptures, church leaders concluded that because the New Testament doesn't talk about using instruments in worship, the Bible prohibits them from being used at all. However, singing is acceptable because the New Testament does talk about singing hymns. So now, this church is non-instrumental and sings everything *a cappella*. By a similar line of logic, many women are convinced that because the Bible doesn't specifically give them permission to wear pants or shorts, they are forbidden from wearing them at all.

With all due respect to my brothers and sisters who holds these beliefs, this is such a harsh way to interpret God's Word. The Old Testament consisted of many laws that the people of Israel had to follow to find favor with God. Jesus came to fulfill the Old Testament law so that we would not be required to keep a bunch of rules to earn God's favor (Matthew 5:17). By creating rules that don't exist on the pages of the Bible, we are holding ourselves back from the freedom that Christ offered us through His sacrifice on the cross. It took the Jewish members of the

33

early New Testament church quite a while to adjust to a life that was guided by the principles of the Law, rather than being obligated to obey every single law. This is something we have to learn to do as well.

The spirit of the new covenant in Christ is freedom, not prohibition, so I believe if the Scriptures are silent on any given topic, we have the freedom to use the principles of Scripture to help us discern what is right and wrong. When it comes to music, even though the New Testament doesn't mention anything about instruments, there is freedom for us to discern how we can use them in worship, as long as nothing that we are doing contradicts anything else that the Scripture teaches.

When it comes to clothes, I believe that God did not want us locked into the social rules of New Testament times in the 21st century. Jesus spent a lot of time breaking some of the social norms of His time because He didn't believe that the people of His day should be stuck having to keep up with the status quo, especially if it is inhibited them from honoring the Lord. One of the reasons I believe He didn't have Paul give a specific order of service or a dress code for worship is because God knew the way that the church worshipped would change with the culture. The Lord wanted to give the church room to adapt to the needs of the world around them. The few times that Paul does have to address the issues with worship or the way they dressed are not meant to hold us to social standards from two thousand years ago. They were meant to be guidelines to help us discern what is right and wrong in our society today. It's important to remember that modesty is meant to be so much more than a list of rules, especially if we are the ones making them up.

3. When We Buy Into the Lies

Mom blogger Stephanie Giese decided she needed to speak up. She loved to shop at Target but was continually frustrated by the length of the shorts they sold for her toddler daughters. So she wrote a blog post as an open letter to Target, showing pictures of how all their girl toddler shorts were so short in length, the crotch was the longest part. She asked that they consider adding length to their girl toddler clothing.[1]

This blog post gained national attention, even being shared by *The Huffington Post*. Although most of the response was positive towards the change she requested, she also received responses, some of which were rather rude, from people who told her they were just toddlers and should expect their clothes to be short. Stephanie decided she needed to prove her point, but this time, she would compare preschool clothing in both boy and girl sizes instead of toddler clothing, documented with pictures.

The results were shocking. She found at both Target and Kohl's that the boy shorts were about seven times longer than the girl shorts of the same size. To get girl shorts of the same length, she had to go up to a large (compared to the boy X-small). The jeans and t-shirts sold to preschool girls were also more fitted, trying to give little girls a figure they don't yet have. She also discovered that while the little girl shorts only had a 1-inch inseam, the women's size 8 shorts had a 2-inch inseam. In other words, according to Target, your inseam should only be an inch longer than the ones on the shorts for your preschool-age daughter.[2] [Both of Stephanie's articles are linked in the back of the book if you want to see the pictures]

It turns out that her second post became just as popular as the first, and Target did begin to affect some changes in the clothes they produced. All because one mother was willing to ask for longer shorts. I remember coming across these posts not long after they became popular. While I was grateful for this woman's courage, I was also shocked by how quickly parents would buy those clothes for their daughters without even thinking about how much they cover. It's a reminder that when it comes to buying clothes off the rack, we should all be a little more careful about trusting what the fashion industry puts in front of us.

A Tale of Caution

At this point, we've talked about several lies we believe about modesty and physical beauty. Hopefully, your eyes have been opened to some of the lies you have believed. However, it's important to not only identify the lies but also to recognize what happens when we accept them as truth. Even though these lies are contemporary in their nature, there is an illustration in Scripture of a woman who gave into some of these lies about beauty and modesty. We are going to take a look at an adulterous woman described in Proverbs 7 and see what she did wrong so that we can avoid finding ourselves in the same place. Let's take a look:

6 For at the window of my house
   I have looked out through my lattice,
7 and I have seen among the simple,
   I have perceived among the youths,
   a young man lacking sense,
8 passing along the street near her corner,
   taking the road to her house

9 in the twilight, in the evening,
   at the time of night and darkness.

10 And behold, the woman meets him,
   dressed as a prostitute, wily of heart.
11 She is loud and wayward;
   her feet do not stay at home;
12 now in the street, now in the market,
   and at every corner she lies in wait.
13 She seizes him and kisses him,
   and with bold face she says to him,
14 "I had to offer sacrifices,
   and today I have paid my vows;
15 so now I have come out to meet you,
   to seek you eagerly, and I have found you.
16 I have spread my couch with coverings,
   colored linens from Egyptian linen;
17 I have perfumed my bed with myrrh,
   aloes, and cinnamon.
18 Come, let us take our fill of love till morning;
   let us delight ourselves with love.
19 For my husband is not at home;
   he has gone on a long journey;
20 he took a bag of money with him;
   at full moon he will come home."

21 With much seductive speech she persuades him;
   with her smooth talk she compels him.
22 All at once he follows her,
   as an ox goes to the slaughter,
or as a stag is caught fast
23 till an arrow pierces its liver;
as a bird rushes into a snare;
   he does not know that it will cost him his life.
(Proverbs 7:6-23 ESV)

Although this is a fictional story by Solomon, we need to take just as much warning from her story as the men he warned. If we don't, we will end up just like her. This woman developed several ungodly traits in her life because she bought into many lies. We're going to take the time to talk about three of them, in hopes that we will not fall into the same traps she did.

WILY OF HEART

This phrase implies that this woman had her heart set on getting her way, regardless of the methods she would have to use to get it. Other translations said she had "crafty intent" or was "cunning of heart." Either way, it gives you a picture of a woman as crafty and manipulative as the serpent in the Garden of Eden. Aside from her evil intentions, what stands out to me about this woman is how self-absorbed she is. She has her heart so set on her desires, she will use any means to get them and any logic to justify them. The argument she makes to seduce the young man is interesting because it's centered on herself. This is the way I summarize her argument: "I've taken care of everything I'm supposed to, so I deserve this. Come to bed with me, because I have a plan since my husband is gone. We can enjoy ourselves and do what we want without consequences because I have it all worked out so no one will know."

If these arguments are starting to sound familiar, they should. This is the heart of a woman who has fully convinced herself of one of the most dangerous lies on our list: I can do whatever I want without consequences. She has become so fully convinced of this lie, she is now willing to betray her husband and deceive innocent young men to fulfill her desires. She goes out of her way to set a trap for them. The passage also mentions that she is wayward and never stays at home, meaning that she probably doesn't fulfill most of her responsibility as a wife. She just likes to wander from party to party to have a good time. She thinks because she's arranged all the details, there will be no consequences for her sin, but nothing could be further from the truth.

The fact that Solomon is using this illustration proves that women like her cannot live however they want without any consequences. If she is not paying the consequences for her sin, someone else is. In this case, it's all the young men she deceived into a metaphoric grave, and her husband if he discovers the truth about her sinful behavior. Even though she thinks she's gotten away with it, her sin will eventually find her out. This is exactly what happens when someone chooses to live for themselves. That is exactly what we should be trying to avoid.

DRESSED TO SEDUCE

Most of the translations of this passage agree that this woman was dressed like a prostitute or harlot. Wearing that kind of clothing makes her intentions obvious: to seduce men. To her, it was just a means for her to get what she wanted. After all, she's convinced herself that she deserves to have fun and find pleasure. Aside from believing that there should be no consequences for her actions, she also bought into the lie that beautiful women are worth more. This means she will use any means to make herself beautiful to the men around her. A woman like her also may have believed that modesty was out of date and needed to catch up with the times. This results in a woman dressed to seduce, just so she can get a man's attention and feel worthy of his affection.

Looking at this woman's example, it's easy to see how quickly we can get sucked into a worldly mindset when it comes to clothes and beauty. Once you buy into one lie, you start to believe more and more of them until the foundation of your identity is built on false ideals. Building up our guard against these lies is crucial if we don't want to end up like her.

LOUD

Although her volume could be considered part of her selfish, crafty heart, I think it's important to discuss separately. According to one of the passages we will talk about later in this book, one of the greatest traits a woman can develop is a gentle and quiet spirit. This woman has the exact opposite: a defiant and loud spirit. Being loud means that you have to make yourself heard above everyone else to get what you want. This is bad enough when accompanied by her sinful behavior, but because she believes lies as truth, she will continue to spread the lies with her increased volume, which will make the world around her more likely to hear and will silence the truth the world needs to hear instead.

One of the reasons these lies are so prevalent is because they are being proclaimed loudly by the secular culture around us and those that have bought into them. Not to mention that many of the Christians who try to contradict them in public are loud and prideful with their rebuttals, which in some ways makes them no better than those spreading the lies. While it's true that we need to find ways to stand up for the truth, we need to learn to do so with quietness and gentility, so that we do not fall into the same trap as the adulterous woman.

Take Warning, Girls

We could break down her ungodly character even further, but hopefully, this is enough to help you see the consequences of building your life on these lies. Just as I said earlier, we need to take just as much warning from this illustration as the men who want to avoid falling into her trap. Believing these lies alters our perception of ourselves, as well as the people around us. It makes us want to live for ourselves and not to the fullness of life that God calls us to through His Son. I believe one of the best ways to find this fullness of life is to embrace modesty as it is laid out in His Word. That's what we are about to discover.

PART 2

Seeking the Truth

4. Keeping the Secret Safe

When I started the seventh grade, I transitioned from homeschooling into a private Christian school. Needless to say, I was pretty nervous. I had been homeschooled since the second grade and didn't know what to expect. It didn't take very long for me to find my way, thanks to my new teacher. One of the things I admired about her so much was that, aside from making sure we got a great education, she called our class her "little disciples," emphasizing that this was more than just a job to her; it was her ministry. I am still receiving the blessings of that ministry today.

One of my favorite lessons I learned from her wasn't even a classroom lesson. It was common around the beginning of the school year to have the "modesty talk" with the female students. They always had a collective one for both junior high and high school girls, but my eighth-grade year, they decided to do a second one with just the junior high girls. At this point, I don't remember too much of what was said in this meeting, but one comment she made has stuck with me ever since she said it. She told us in her sweet little Alabaman accent: "Remember girls, as Gandalf said in *The Lord of the Rings*,

'Keep it secret, keep it safe.' "

Needless to say, we all laughed so hard! People still laugh when I share that story today. In the end, although this comment was meant to be humorous, it also made a powerful point. To understand the point she was making, I want to briefly summarize the plot of *The Lord of the Rings*.

The evil Dark Lord named Sauron created the Ring of Power many years ago, a ring that would allow him to rule all of Middle-earth. When Frodo the hobbit is given a gold ring by his cousin Bilbo, the wise wizard Gandalf suspects it's the Ring of Power. To see if his suspicions were true, Gandalf had to leave immediately to do some research in a kingdom far away (in the film version, at least). Frodo was very confused. Gandalf had only arrived earlier that day and Frodo didn't understand why he had to leave so soon, but Gandalf knew that they could not take any chances until they found the truth. That's why he declared (in both the film and the book), "Keep it secret, and keep it safe!"[1]

When Gandalf told Frodo this, Frodo had no idea what the Ring was, the power it had, or the potential danger it posed for him to have it in his possession. For that matter, Gandalf was not entirely sure himself, but until they were sure, Frodo could not take any chances. Gandalf instructed him to keep the Ring hidden, telling no one he had it, and to guard it securely, ensuring no one could steal it. When Gandalf returned, his research had confirmed that Frodo had the Ring of Power, which would send the hobbit on a great journey to destroy the Ring.

The line "keep it secret, keep it safe" has stuck with me ever since that modesty talk when I was fourteen years old. It's funny to think that something you heard at that age would stick with you, but as a Lord of the Rings fan, it was humorous and it made sense. As I got older and learned more about what the Bible teaches about modesty, I appreciated this analogy more and more. Men and women alike have also been given a power, although in our case, it doesn't come from a gold ring. Understanding this power and how we should use it is crucial to living a lifestyle of modesty.

The Significance of this Power

The first passage we are going to discuss here may surprise you that this is even in the Bible, or that I am publically sharing about this in a book. Regardless, we are going to use this passage to do two things: to help women understand the minds of men and to help us understand the way that God designed our bodies. Let's take a look at Proverbs 5:18-19:

"May your fountain be blessed, and may you rejoice in the wife of your youth. A loving doe, a graceful deer— may her breasts satisfy you always, may you ever be captivated by her love." (NIV)

As I said earlier, some of you may be shocked that I chose to share this verse with you. Even though some of this wording seems blunt, this translation is a toned-down version of the original meaning of the Greek words.[2] So let's look at vs. 19 again, but this time in the ESV.

"Let her breasts fill you at all times with delight; be intoxicated always in her love." (ESV)

Intoxicated? Now that is strong wording! This verse tells us that our bodies have the power to intoxicate a man with our beauty. It's pretty incredible for us to realize that God designed us that way. This power should be seen as an incredible gift to be used in the right way at the right time. The problem is that most of us are either unaware of how great this power is or we use our knowledge of this power to bring attention to ourselves. As Christian women, our goal should be to save the deepest secrets of our beauty for the man we marry.[2] It should be vice versa for Christian men – they should be saving the deepest secrets of their manhood for just one woman – their wife.

1 Timothy 2:9-10

The reason that many people within the church are resistant to the concept of modesty is that there is a collective misunderstanding of what the Bible says about it. This needs to change. We all need to take the time to understand what the Bible tells us about what we should wear, so we can shape our lives in response to it. So I want to take a look at 1 Timothy 2. This is the only direct reference to the word that translates as "modesty" in the New Testament and is usually the first passage referenced when discussing the topic.

"...women should adorn themselves in respectable apparel, with modesty and self-control not with braided hair and gold or pearls or costly attire, but with what is proper for women who profess godliness – with good works" (ESV)

Now is anyone confused by any of the language and cultural references here? To be honest, they confuse me and I've graduated from a Bible college! I think that this is one of the main reasons why this passage is avoided: we don't know how to adapt the cultural references into a contemporary context. So that's exactly what we are going to do. We're going to go through the five points that this passage teaches us about how women were supposed to dress back then, so we can learn how we should dress now.

1. We Should Adorn Ourselves

First and foremost, Paul says that women should adorn themselves. Remember how I shared earlier that some women use the words "frumpy and dumpy" to describe modesty? I think this passage tells us otherwise. The word that is used for "adorn" here could be defined as making something beautiful. Now, I'm not saying that we need to plaster on the makeup and wear formal clothes all the time, but I do think that this passage tells us that we should put some effort into our appearance, especially on Sundays at church. It's a great reminder that sometimes, not putting effort into your appearance can be just as much of a distraction as putting too much effort into your appearance. It's important to learn the difference between too much and not enough.

2. WE SHOULD ADORN OURSELVES APPROPRIATELY

This passage also says that we need to be adorned in respectable apparel. The word "respectable" could be translated as modest, proper, suitable, or appropriate. Through my study of the Scriptures, what I believe this is talking about is about learning to dress in a manner that is always "appropriate to the occasion." This is a phrase I coined that I believe fits best with the concept that this Scripture is teaching here about clothing and modesty. Here are a few questions to illustrate how it works:

Would you want to wear sweatpants and a t-shirt to prom?
Would you wear a prom dress on a regular school day?
Would you wear a swimsuit for a job interview?

If you answered "no" to all these questions, you are right! This is because none of these clothing options are appropriate for the given situation. "Appropriate to the occasion" means learning to have a social awareness about what is appropriate to wear in any and every situation. Some situations, like the ones listed above, are no-brainers. Other situations are not as obvious. For example, if you chose to go on a missions trip to a foreign country, you would probably need to do some research to determine if any of the clothes you plan to bring would be considered inappropriate in that country. We need to learn to do this in our own country too. We have to learn to be thinking ahead to what is appropriate in each situation specifically because it shows respect and honor to those around us.

3. We Should Adorn Ourselves with Self-Control

Next, we are told that we should be adorned with modesty and self-control. The ESV uses these words side-by-side, and I don't think it's a coincidence. The word for "self-control," aside from implying moderation, also can be translated as "sound judgment" or "sound mind." This means that you are to have the discernment to know what is right and wrong and then use your sound judgment to choose to do what is right.

When you know you have the power to attract attention to yourself with your appearance, it takes sound judgment to not use that power selfishly. You have to learn how to intentionally hold back from showing off your body so that you are not a distraction and so you can save yourself for the person you will marry. Learning how to develop sound judgment about the clothes you wear begins with studying His Word. This and other passages in the Scriptures show us principles about clothing and behaviors we should avoid. When you learn these Scripture and take their wisdom to heart, having sound judgment in any situation will become second nature to you.

4. We Shouldn't Adorn Ourselves in Vanity and Worldly Wealth

Vanity is being too focused on your physical appearance. This includes your clothes, but also on your hair, your makeup, your complexion, and even your body image. When you are more concerned with the way you look on Sundays than you are about the sermon, you have not only missed the point, but you run the risk of becoming a distraction to those around you. You then exchange the sound judgment you're supposed to have for bad judgment that often leads to compromise.

We are also not to get caught up in worldly wealth. Braids, gold, pearls, and costly attire were all ways that women of the early church would display their wealth or social status. These women were trying to make themselves feel more important than the women of lower class. Their appearance became a distraction and proved to be an inappropriate way to dress, especially in a setting of home churches. Even if they were not showing cleavage or their legs, their fancy up-dos, their bright-colored robes, and all their shiny bling were a distraction for those trying to worship the Lord. A church service is not an appropriate place to draw that kind of attention to yourself. It wasn't appropriate in the first century and it's still not appropriate today. That's part of the reason why it's so important that what we wear is appropriate for each given situation.

As I mentioned earlier, I am a big Disney fan. My favorite movie of all time is Disney's animated classic *Beauty and the Beast*. One of the things I have always wanted is an authentic replica of Belle's yellow dress in my size. Just imagine what would happen if my dream came true and I was so excited about getting this dress that I decided to wear the large, yellow, puffy dress, along with the matching accessories and up-do, to a church service. What do you think would happen? It would be a *huge* distraction. People would spend more time watching me than singing the songs or listening to the sermon. Even if my dress wasn't inappropriate, it would be meant to draw too much attention to myself and that would make it immodest. That is what we have to learn to avoid.

5. We Should Adorn Ourselves with Good Works (Godliness)

Instead of adorning ourselves in wealth and vanity, we are to adorn ourselves with the kinds of actions that bring glory to God, so that we in the process are adorned with godliness. The word "modest" here implies reverence or honor, not only for God, but also for rulers, parents, and others worthy of respect. The way we live our lives should be a continual act of worship to the Lord. We should be adorned with godliness, the good works we do that will point people back to the God whom we profess to worship.

One of my favorite teachings on this passage is by David Platt, author of the book *Radical*. In a longer sermon about 1 Timothy 2, he spends about 7 minutes discussing the biblical concept of modesty. [Link to full sermon available in the back of the book] Of all of the things he said in that sermon, one quote stands out from the rest:

"Let us raise up women across this church that get up every day, including Sunday, thinking humbly, 'How can I dress today and what can I do today that will draw the most attention to the glory of my God?' That's not easy in today's culture. That's totally against the grain."[3]

I love how this question gets to the heart of biblical modesty. We need to live our lives in such a way that we are not trying to draw unnecessary attention to ourselves. The One we are taking attention away from when we dress this way is the God we worship. We were made to be His creation and to bring glory back to Him. We're going to take about how to make that happen in the next chapter.

5. It's What's Inside That Counts

One of the problems I see with the way modesty is addressed in many churches is that it is almost exclusively based on the clothes you wear. Although some churches get it right, others struggle with making it all about the rules without addressing the heart attitude. The truth is that attitude is everything when it comes to modesty. Most of us don't think of it that way, but it remains true:

The way that you dress reflects the condition of your heart.

This concept really should make you think twice when you get dressed in the morning. Your outward presentation reflects what's happening inside your heart. This means that there may be times when a woman may be appropriately covered, but because she still has an unhealthy desire for attention, she has an immodest attitude. In moments when I encounter young women like this, it grieves me to see them reflecting the struggles of their hearts in their clothing choices. This is why it's important to make sure your insides match your outsides.

THE PRETTY BOY WHO WOULDN'T BE KING

Before we dive into the main passage for this chapter, I want to take a look at a story about when one of God's prophets had to learn a lesson about physical beauty. Samuel would be the last of the judges that reigned over Israel when they were governed by a theocracy, a form of government with God as their king and human judges as

God's spokesman. But the people insisted on having a "real" king so that they could be like the nations around them. Samuel was upset that they wouldn't listen to God, but God assured Samuel that it would be alright and that He would reveal the right man to Samuel. The man God chose was named Saul. Through a series of events, Saul and one of his father's servants found themselves in the same town as Samuel and God revealed that this man was meant to be king. Samuel probably knew Saul was king material from the first time he looked at him. The Scriptures tell us that Saul was tall and handsome (1 Samuel 9:2). Anointing him probably seemed like a no-brainer. God said Saul would be the one to save Israel from the Philistines. It all sounded very promising.

However, it didn't take very long for King Saul to stop listening to the Lord's instruction. On more than one occasion, Saul only obeyed part of the Lord's commands instead of all of them. He started trying to solve problems on his own and do things his way. After multiple offenses and warnings, Samuel declared that the Lord had rejected Saul as king and would choose another to take his place. Eventually, the Lord would send Samuel to see Jesse of Bethlehem to choose one of his sons to anoint as the next king of Israel. To make sure that Saul would not discover his plan, God told Samuel to invite Jesse and his sons to offer a sacrifice with him. As they were doing so, Samuel saw Jesse's oldest son, Eliab. Samuel thought for sure that he would be the Lord's anointed. But God said to him,

"Do not look on his appearance or on the height of his stature, because I have rejected him. For the Lord sees not as man sees: man looks on the outward appearance, but the Lord looks at the heart." (1 Samuel 16:7 ESV)

At the end of the day, after seeing seven of Jesse's sons, Samuel asked to see the youngest. When David arrived, straight from the fields with the herds, the Lord confirmed that he would be the Lord's anointed. It's interesting to note that although David was described as having beautiful eyes, he was also described as being "ruddy," or reddish, in appearance. I believe that David didn't immediately strike Samuel's eye as being king material, especially since Saul had been tall and handsome. I think that's part of the reason that the Lord had to essentially tell Samuel, "I'm picking this man for his heart, not his appearance. Be prepared, because this guy might not be much to look at."

We live in a world where we judge everyone and everything by external appearances, but in this story, we learn that God doesn't judge a book by its cover. He cares more about our hearts being in line with His will than He does about our physical appearance. Saul might have been easy on the eyes, but he didn't have his heart in line with the Lord. David, on the other hand, may not have been much to look at as a ruddy shepherd, but he had the heart willing to do what God asked of him. He later became remembered as a man after God's own heart. Like David, if your heart is in the right place, that makes you beautiful to God, no matter what anyone else says.

1 Peter 3:3-4

If this is a struggle for most women, how can we have the right attitude that will lead us to the right wardrobe choices? Fortunately, there is a passage in the Bible that helps us figure out how to do this. We are going to walk through 1 Peter 3:3-4, which teaches us that what's on the inside is what matters most.

"Do not let your adorning be external—the braiding of hair and the putting on of gold jewelry, or the clothing you wear — but let your adorning be the hidden person of the heart with the imperishable beauty of a gentle and quiet spirit, which in God's sight is very precious." (ESV)

I think this passage reveals three things we must learn. Let's take a look:

1. Don't Focus on the Outside

As it was in the 1 Timothy passage, the women of the New Testament church were discouraged from using hairdos, jewelry, and fancy robes to display their social status. This doesn't mean that we are forbidden from wearing these things, but it does mean that they shouldn't be the primary source of our outward adornment.

The word used for adorn in this passage is a different word than we discussed in 1 Timothy. Interestingly, the word used for adorn in this passage, although it is translated to mean "ornament", could also be translated as "world". I think this can take on a double meaning. Our world and the person we are should not be defined by our hairstyles, our accessories, or our clothing. All of that, in the end, is superficial and will not bring us value or satisfaction.

Jesus himself warned about the dangers of being too concerned with outward appearances. In Matthew 23, Jesus addressed Pharisees who struggled with dressing up the outside but ignoring their heart condition. He tells them in verse 26, "First clean the inside of the cup and the plate, that the outside also may be clean."(ESV) This is something that we all need to learn to do, or we will be just as blind as the Pharisees.

2. Focus on the Inside

Instead of focusing on the outside, our adorning should be defined by the beauty of our inner qualities. I absolutely love the wording "hidden person of the heart". This is the person we are deep down inside. I believe that these qualities of inner beauty are inside of every woman who has ever lived. It's the way God made us. However, there are times when we ignore these inner qualities and chose instead to do things our way, making both our inner character and our outer beauty reflect this conflict. We must do our best to remember that even when it's hard to have the right attitude, God has given us the ability and strength to find that spirit within our hearts. I will get back to the "imperishable" part in just a minute. I want to spend some time concentrating on the way that inner beauty is described: A gentle and quiet spirit.

First, we are told to find a gentle spirit. Some of the other words used to describe gentle include humble, mild, and meek. I don't want to get too caught up in definitions here, but I think that some of the things that are included in a gentle spirit are patience, kindness, and humility. I have heard several different married men talk about their wives having a gentle spirit when exhorting him. The description is pretty consistent among all these stories: her kindness and gentility convicts and humbles him of his selfishness and pride. It makes him want to change his ways to be a better husband and father. That is the very quality I think we all need to find, a gentleness that is honest but kind when it needs to be, so we can speak the truth in love. It should be a gentility that draws people back to God.

Second, we are told to find a quiet spirit. Unfortunately, many women in today's culture are the exact opposite of quiet, just like the adulterous woman in Proverbs 7. In a culture that values loud women, expressing their opinions whenever and however they want, we must learn the art of discerning when we need to just stop talking. This will be so our words will be better received when we do speak, and so our words can reflect a heart that honors the Lord.

This is much easier said than done. I tend to have a voice that doesn't struggle to be heard. When I was a cheerleader in high school or even now when I'm in a crowded room trying to get someone's attention, this is not a problem. However, when I get excited in normal conversation, I can sometimes hurt people's ears by accidentally increasing my volume (sorry Mom and Dad!). So one of the things I am trying to learn to do in my own life is to listen more. We tend to get so caught up in what we want to say and do in a noisy world, that we don't stop to listen to what God or others may be saying that we need to hear. This makes me think of Mary, sister of Martha and Lazarus, sitting quietly at the feet of Jesus while Martha was busy in the kitchen (Luke 10:38-41). When Martha gets upset, Jesus tells Martha that while she was worried about many things, Mary got the one essential thing right: a quiet spirit, ready to listen to Jesus.

Being gentle and quiet is not easy in today's culture, with so many women that have attitudes and egos the size of the Statue of Liberty, living for themselves and not taking into consideration how to honor God or their neighbor. However, I believe every woman on this earth can find a gentle and quiet spirit within their heart. God made them that way, but some have chosen to ignore that nature. As Christian women who desire to honor the Lord with the way we present ourselves, we must choose to be gentle and quiet in a loud and abrasive world.

One of the best parts about it is that the beauty in this quietness and gentility won't go away. The word imperishable can be translated as "unfading" or "immortal". Unlike beauty methods that will make us beautiful for only a day at a time, the beauty of this spirit, should we choose to cultivate it, will never fade. It will last with us into eternity. I remember a conversation I had with a group of friends in college. One of the girls commented on getting the "eternity headache". This is when you are trying to think about the scope of eternity and just when you think you maybe have your head around it, you get a headache. We laughed about it but realized that she had a good point. We think we understand the scope of eternity, but we can't within our human minds. Knowing that the beauty that He created within my soul will last into eternity is humbling, to say the least. Since I hope to be spending my eternity praising and honoring the Lord, I want to develop the type of spirit that can do this now. And I hope you do too.

3. Focus on Your Worth

The last thing we should take from this passage is that not only should we adorn ourselves with a beautiful spirit, but that we also should adorn ourselves in the love and worth God has for us. The NIV says that having this spirit is of great worth in God's sight. The ESV says that it is precious in God's sight. The word used here could also be translated as "valuable". God gave us the ability to choose this kind of spirit because we are valuable and precious in His sight. You are His creation and He considers you to be

His masterpiece. He takes pride in you and delights in you. He wants to have a relationship with you. He loves you more than you will ever be able to comprehend. The value that He has given you is the ultimate reason that this inner beauty will never fade away.

One of my favorite reminders of this is a YouTube video called "Who You Are – A Message to All Women." This video, although it was incredibly simple in its concept, is very powerful in its message. It's a reminder that despite our insecurities, we can find our value in the One who created us and calls us His daughter. Knowing that gives us the ability to find the beautiful spirit He gave us, not only of quietness and gentility but also of strength.[1] [Link available in the back of the book]

Choosing to maintain that perspective will keep you from dwelling on yourself and your appearance and will instead help you focus on Him and His Word. It will also prepare your heart to yield to whatever He has in store for you, which will probably be greater than anything you could have ever imagined for yourself. Before we get there, we're going to need to go back to the foot of the cross.

6. Bought With a Price

Almost every girl loves a good chick flick, especially the ones that can be classified as romantic comedies. They love the couple's witty banter because it's a sign that they are meant to be together. They love to follow the ups and downs of these characters' relationships, sometimes even ignoring the fact that these relationships are unhealthy. Too often, we love the "happily ever after" that Hollywood promises, but we realize that what's portrayed on the screen reflects versions of romance and relationships that usually lead to disappointment and brokenness. This is the main reason that this genre of modern film is one of my least favorites to watch.

However, there a specific type of romantic drama that I enjoy seeing portrayed more than any other: the one where the man has to fight for the woman he loves. Whether it be a physical fight, needing to save her from danger, or emotionally fighting to win her heart, these are the best kind of romances. Sometimes, the story will result in both the man and the woman fighting for each other, but the loyalty of the man is especially powerful and compelling. My favorite among all of these is a unique class of romance, the ones where the man loves the woman so much that he sacrifices himself for her sake. There is nothing that will move me more emotionally than a story where I know the guy is giving up his life for the woman he loves.

There are usually two endings to this scenario. The Disney version results in some sort of magic healing of the man or reversal of his fate. Sometimes, they think he's dead or he believes he will die, but he miraculously survives. In both of these cases, the result is a "happily ever after," with a love stronger than it was before. The other version, the one you don't usually see in Disney films, is sad but also powerful. This is the one where the guy dies and stays dead, but the woman becomes a better, more complete version of herself because of all that she learned and experienced with him. She often falls in love with someone else down the road, if the story continues that far. She doesn't forget the man that gave up everything for her, but she does find the freedom to live her life to the fullest as a result of his sacrifice.

Even as I am describing these scenes, you probably remember some of your favorite movies that have similar scenes. Since I do not want to spoil the plot of movies you may not have seen, I will only share one example. As I have mentioned previously, my favorite movie of all time is Disney's *Beauty and the Beast*. I believe this to be the perfect example of this type of story that nearly everyone has seen. (If you haven't, I highly recommend you put this book down and go watch either the 1991 animated version or the 2017 live-action version. Seriously. Go do it right now and then come back.) What I love so much about this romance compared to many others is that their story wasn't love at first sight. Instead, they had to learn to love each other, and that love changed them both. They were willing to sacrifice everything for each other. Beast was willing to sacrifice his humanity for the sake of Belle and her father, and Belle was willing to risk her life to save Beast. It was by these sacrifices that they realized they loved each other. Their love not only saved each other but also saved the prince's entire household from their imprisonment.

When I watch these scenes and other scenes like them, through the tears of emotion I sometimes experience, I have one thought that consistently pops into my head: *I wish I had a man that loved me that much.* I'm sure I'm not the only one who's had this thought. I think it's essentially hardwired into women's brains to desire that kind of sacrificial love for ourselves. Especially for those of us who are single, we find that watching these kinds of scenes makes us desire it all the more.

If we want to learn how to satisfy this longing, I need to take you back to a story we already talked about earlier in this book: Adam and Eve in the Garden of Eden.

The Story of the Gospel

In the beginning, after creating light, water, land, vegetation, and all kinds of creatures, God saw it was good, but He realized that something was missing. So He made His most precious creation: man. Even then, He knew this creation was incomplete, so He also created a woman to be a companion and mate to the man. This is when He knew His creation was truly complete and said it was very good (Genesis 1:31). He loved the man and woman more than anything else within His creation and lived in unity with them. He gave them dominion over the land and the animals and told them to fill the earth with their offspring (Genesis 1:28). They only had one rule: don't eat fruit from that one tree. This perfection was all that they could imagine and more.

Unfortunately, this perfect life would not last long, because they chose to break their one rule. When they did, they knew the difference between right and wrong. The first thing they realized was that they were naked, and they felt the weight of that shame. At first, all they could think to do was make clothes out of fig leaves to cover up their shame (Genesis 3:7). When God realized what had happened, He rebuked their disobedience, but He also had compassion on them in their sinful state. Instead of leaving them in their insufficient coverings, He killed an animal to make them better clothing out of its skin (Genesis 3:21). This sacrifice and the clothing He made for them would serve as a foreshadowing of God's plan to bring mankind, now separated from Him by sin, back to Himself.

For thousands of years, God would slowly fulfill His plan through His chosen people, all while watching His people do what was right in their own eyes and turn away from Him. Some men shared fellowship with Him, but it was nothing like His fellowship in the Garden with Adam and Eve. Although He would become angry with His people for their disobedience, He also took compassion on them, even when their unfaithfulness continued. He longed to be one in spirit with them, knowing that the way would be made ready soon.

Finally, a little boy was born to a virgin mother and was prophesied to be the Son of God Himself. He showed compassion to the people in their sinful state. He spent three years teaching the way of the Lord and training His disciples in that way. Sadly, as it had been with many of the prophets God had sent before Him, the right people hardened their hearts towards Him. After being betrayed by a close friend, He was handed over to His enemies, who wrongfully accused Him and ordered His execution.

This execution in many ways mirrored the sacrifice that God made for Adam and Eve in the Garden. In both cases, God knew someone had to pay the penalty for the sins that had been committed. For Adam and Eve, it was an innocent animal who had done no wrong. This animal had to give up its life so Adam and Eve could find their way back to God. For the rest of us, an even greater sacrifice was required. This sacrifice was meant to cover every person for every sin they've ever committed. Any old sacrifice simply wouldn't do. Not even the purest of all animals would be sufficient. So God sent down His Son, a part of Himself, to be the ultimate sacrifice for our sins. Just like Adam and Eve were covered by grace as a result of the sacrifice God made for them, we are also covered with grace by the sacrifice that Jesus made for us.

Returning to the Foot of the Cross

Have you ever slowed down to meditate on the phrase "Jesus died for me"? This phrase is one of the most essential truths of the Christian faith, but I think we often lose sight of it in the middle of the difficulties of life. We have all heard that Jesus died on the cross, but I think because He only remained dead for three days, we can tend to forget that He died in the first place. This should not be. The truth remains that He endured the most physically agonizing execution of His time for the sake of our salvation.

He was beaten, slapped, and spit upon multiple times. He was flogged with whips that had pieces of glass and broken pottery embedded in the leather, which would have destroyed the skin on his back to the point that the muscles and sinews would have been exposed.[1] He had a crown of sharp thorns shoved on His head, causing further blood loss. This left Him so weak that He collapsed under the weight of the cross that He was forced to carry. He was so disfigured, He was hardly recognizable as human (Isaiah 52:14), and this was all before He was put on the cross.

They nailed Him through the bones of His wrists and ankles, then mounted Him on the cross. Then He would have had to push himself up against His shredded back using His spiked hands and feet just to take a breath. After about six hours, He would die of asphyxiation (aka suffocation), not to mention that while on the cross, He would bear the emotional pain of being separated from the Heavenly Father, and would also be emotionally reeling from being betrayed by His disciples, especially Judas and Peter.

Some people try to claim that while Jesus was on the cross, He was thinking of you specifically. I don't believe this to be true. I think that He was thinking about Judas, a close friend who committed the deepest betrayal for money, and would pay the ultimate price. He was thinking about Peter, who in the moment of truth lost his backbone and denied Jesus, which he swore he would never do. He was thinking about His other disciples who, all except John, had abandoned Him in His hour of greatest need. He was thinking about those who mocked and beat Him. Even amid His suffering, He asked God to forgive the sins they didn't even know they were committing. Although the Scriptures don't tell us, I think He may have asked God to forgive Judas, Peter, and all the others who ran away, even though they knew they were betraying Him. That's what His mind was focused on while He was on the cross: redeeming all who had turned against Him from their sin.

Remember how I referenced the thought I often have when watching a guy sacrificing himself? When I remember the cross, I realize that I do have a man who loved me enough to die for me. Even though I have sinned and done so many things to disown Him, He still died for my ransom. When I take time to reflect on this truth, it changes the way I see myself and the way I see everyone around me.

I want to encourage you to take a few moments right now to meditate on what Jesus did for you on the cross. Find a place where you can be alone, just you and God. Take the opportunity to reread these last few paragraphs to allow the story to become embedded in your memory. If you can look up music or video, look up three songs: "Why" by Nicole Nordeman, "Who Am I" by Casting Crowns, and "Someone Worth Dying For" by MIKESCHAIR. Listen to them in that order. [Link to YouTube playlist is available in the back of the book]

POWERFUL REMINDERS

"Why" tells a fictional story about a little girl who witnesses the crucifixion of Jesus. The little girl asks why this man that her dad admired had to be treated so cruelly. Jesus in turn, asks God why he had to go through all of this pain and humiliation. God answers, but replies that He can't do anything to spare Him from the pain. God explains that His blood would redeem the lies and that this little girl that witnessed his death was the reason why He had to die.[2] Although I believe that Jesus fully grasped the reasons for His death before He was crucified, this song paints a powerful word picture of what it would have been like to witness this event, as well as some of the emotions that Jesus and God were probably experiencing.

"Who Am I" is a reminder of how small we are in the grand scheme of life. However, we are aware of how much the God of the universe loves and pursues us. The singer is choosing to be aware that it's not because of who he is that God cares. It's all because of who God is that He chose to redeem us from our sin and continues to pursue us. It ends with the simple declaration "I am yours."[3]

"Someone Worth Dying For" is a reminder that even amid the difficulties of this life, we can remember the price that Jesus paid for our ransom. Even if you think that you could never deserve the grace that is offered to you, you are beautiful and precious in the sight of our Lord and Savior. He loved you enough to die for you, and every other person that would ever receive Him. You can never earn it, but it's by this precious gift that you can know your worth and your purpose.[4]

All three of these songs have played a significant role in my spiritual life. The first two were performed by my school choir the night I was baptized. The three songs together paint a powerful picture of our value in God's eyes, which will also change our view of ourselves.

MODESTY AND THE GOSPEL

By now, you are probably wondering "What do chick flicks and Jesus dying on the cross have to do with how we dress?" The answer is everything! Another detail about the crucifixion is that many scholars believe that Jesus was naked when He was crucified. Pretty much all the artwork and film versions of the crucifixion portray Him wearing what I call the "Jesus diaper". I understand why they do this (and am quite grateful that they do), but we often forget that in that culture, they didn't wear undergarments. They wore an outer robe and an inner robe with no additional protection underneath, and since the Scripture tells us that the soldiers were casting lots for his inner robe (John 19:23-24), Jesus probably had no clothes on while on the cross.[5]

I believe there is a powerful truth here. Jesus endured the shame of public nakedness, not only for the redemption of our sins but to ensure that none of us have to expose ourselves to earn the approval of men. If you know that your worth was defined at the foot of the cross, you will realize that you don't have to wear what everyone else is wearing to find acceptance and worth. Jesus already took care of that so that we wouldn't have to find our worth from sources that will never satisfy, like the approval of others. Paul reminds us of this in 1 Corinthians:

"Do you not know that your body is a temple of the Holy Spirit within you, whom you have from God? You are not your own, for you were bought with a price. So glorify God in your body." (1 Corinthians 6:19-20 ESV)

This passage is talking about sexual immorality, which as we have already discussed, is very much related to modesty. These verses make such a powerful point. If you have accepted Christ as your personal Lord and Savior, then you have received the gift of the Holy Spirit. Therefore, Paul is concluding that your body is a temple where the Spirit of God dwells freely and should be treated accordingly.

In this passage, Paul delivers one of the most powerful lines in all the Scriptures: "You are not your own, for you were bought with a price." Even though we have been discussing Jesus' death, I don't think that most of us think of ourselves as "bought with a price", but we should. To Jesus, you are priceless and were worthy of the ultimate sacrifice – His life. To Him, you were worth dying for. That truth, in and of itself, should cause all of us to fall on our knees in humble gratitude every day of our lives, and cause us to never again doubt our value in God's eyes.

But this verse also says, "You are not your own". Since we receive our salvation as a gift, we still owe a debt we could never repay. We've already talked about how God doesn't want us to feel obligated to keep a bunch of rules to earn His favor. I think this passage is encouraging us to realize that if we believe and are grateful for what Jesus did for us on the cross, we will naturally desire to honor Him with what we do with our bodies. This desire will not come out of a place of obligation, but out of a place of thanksgiving and gratitude. If you pay attention to nothing else in this book, then please pay attention to this:

If you really believe that Jesus died for you, then you are going to want to dress like Jesus died for you

This desire will come out of a place of gratitude over all the Lord has done in your life, not out of an obligation to keep a list of rules. You will genuinely desire to bring attention to God or the good works of others in the way that you present yourself. You will want to dress like you believe you are redeemed by the blood of Christ. It wouldn't be about hiding your body or avoiding sin, but it will become part of a lifestyle that does its best to worship God in all areas of life.

7. Known by Our Fruit

If we are able to take the hope of our salvation to heart, then we are going to start reflecting this hope in the way we live our daily lives. It will become about so much more than the way that we dress. When our gratitude motivates us to live to honor Christ, then we begin to learn other character traits that the Scripture teaches as a result. These character traits should become what attracts the people around us to our lives and our faith. Hopefully, these people will start saying to themselves, "There's something different about them. I want what they have". These traits, which the Scriptures also call virtues, are how we are to be clothed, not in vanity or worldly wealth.

The New Testament uses the metaphor of bearing good fruit to help us understand these virtues. Whether we realize it or not, all the decisions we make and attitudes we have bear fruit, just like trees bear fruit. If the character traits we have are dishonoring the Lord or are self-centered, then we are bearing bad fruit. Only the traits we develop or decisions we make that glorify the Lord or put others ahead of ourselves produce good fruit. Therefore, we are encouraged through God's Word to develop the traits that bear good fruit and avoid bearing bad fruit.

Most Christian know the Fruit of the Spirit. They are meant to be the outward signs of inner beauty, which is part of the gentle and quiet spirit we are supposed to develop. Since we know that we are to be known by these virtues, we are going to take a brief look at each one. Some of these traits have already been discussed, which makes it all the more important to pay attention to their significance to our spiritual lives. Let's take a look at the Fruit of the Spirit:

"But the fruit of the Spirit is love, joy, peace, patience, kindness, goodness, faithfulness, gentleness, self-control; against such things there is no law." (Galatians 5:22-23 ESV)

LOVE

Love is a word that is often overused in our culture. It's fairly common knowledge that many other languages have multiple words for love, while the English language has only one. In the Greek of the New Testament, there were four words for love, three of which were used in the New Testament itself. The one used here is the most common word for love, *agape*. It's sometimes translated as "charity." What makes this word incredible is that it is the word used to describe the love that God has for us, the love that compelled Jesus to die on the cross for our sins. It's a sacrificial love that puts someone else's needs before your own. With this trait being at the top of the list, it's the foundation for all the other traits that follow.

JOY

Many people associate the word "joy" with happiness. While it's true that happiness can be a part of the concept of joy, the type of joy that is described in the Scriptures can be present even when you aren't happy. Even when you are facing your most difficult circumstances, you can still find joy in remembering all that Jesus has done for you. Not only is this a huge part of our motivation for dressing modestly, but it also can be our greatest motivation to find contentment when life doesn't make sense. If we can learn to be grateful in all circumstances, we can learn to find joy.

PEACE

While a lot of people would try to define peace as the absence of worry, the Greek word used here could be translated as "freedom from worry." This passage is a reminder that, even if the things that worry us never go away, we can find freedom by putting our trust in the One who loved us enough to die for us. We can choose to not be imprisoned by our worries. Jesus reminds us that worry won't add a single hour to our lives, but choosing to seek the Lord despite our worries will ensure that the Lord will take care of us (Matthew 6:27, 33). Laying all of our worries down at the feet of Jesus is the best way to find freedom from them.

PATIENCE

Patience, sometimes translated as "forbearance", is the ability to wait for something to happen. Sometimes, it includes withholding something until the right time, but either way, it can be defined as the ability to wait well. This trait is hard to cultivate in a culture of instant gratification, but a patient person is willing to recognize the rewards that will come by waiting for what they want.

Having this trait also means learning to bear with those who make patience difficult or repeat their mistakes, like the type of person we talked about in this book's introduction. That can be quite difficult, as we want to just change their flaws so we don't have to deal with them. In many of those cases, I've found that God has more to teach me through being patient with them than He has to teach them. It's about our willingness to bear with and forgive their offenses, just as Christ has forgiven us.

Kindness

Kindness is a trait that many know but struggle to practice. It is usually associated with having an agreeable or nice personality and genuine concern for the needs of others. It's not always easy to have an agreeable personality, especially when the circumstances of life are difficult, but I think the key is focusing on the needs of others more than on your own circumstances. Being filled with compassion for their struggles and their needs helps you to realize how blessed you are, and that, in turn, will make you a more pleasant person to be around.

Goodness

I think that goodness can often be confused with kindness. In this case, I am going to focus on another word that distinguishes it from kindness: generosity. It's kind of like the saying "giving out of the goodness of their heart". This is when you willingly give of your resources to help fulfill the needs of others, especially your money or your time. While it's true that not everyone has the spiritual gift of generosity, we are all called to contribute to the needs of others and not ignore a need when we see it. Choosing to give to someone or something you believe in, especially when there is no gain for you, is one of the noblest things a person can do.

Faithfulness

I think this word can be interpreted in a few different ways. Within the context of this passage, this virtue is about being dependable or trustworthy. Aside from striving to stay faithful to the Lord or faithful to a spouse, we also need to become the friend that others can depend on during their most difficult times. This is the kind of friend that not only shares in life and fellowship with you but also the friend who will stick by you when things get tough, even if it means showing tough love.

Everyone wants to be the friend that sticks with you, but the real sign of genuine faithfulness is when you do what is best for the other person, even if it damages the friendship. This quality is such an important part of living life in Christian community, but it isn't always applied to the concept of friendships. It's important for Christian women to know that we have sisters in Christ to comfort and support us when we are going through hard times, but we also need to learn how to be that sister when someone else needs it.

GENTLENESS

We've already talked about the importance of developing a gentle spirit in 1 Peter 3, but one concept that is related to the Greek word here is worth discussing: courtesy. Aside from avoiding coming across abrasively, another aspect of gentleness is being polite and courteous to those around us. It can be hard to be gentle to those that are abrasive, rude, or inconsiderate. We tend to think that our abrasiveness will solve their own. Instead, we should resolve to be gentle in a harsh world, which will make us stand out from the crowd.

SELF-CONTROL

We've already discussed self-control in 1 Timothy 2, although it is worth noting that the Greek word used here is different from 1 Timothy. While Timothy talked about having sound judgment, the word in this passage suggests the concept of mastery. While the other word encourages control over your thoughts, this word emphasizes control over your actions. Having control over both our thoughts and actions is important to our walk with the Lord. After all, it's hard to have control over our actions if we can't control our thoughts. Both will start with having a sound mind and building up the wisdom to discern what is right and wrong. Then you will know what you need to do to best honor the Lord when temptation comes.

8. Clothed in Virtue

The Fruit of the Spirit are not to be the only virtues that should clothe us. There is even a verse that tells us other virtues that should clothe God's people:

Therefore, as God's chosen people, holy and dearly loved, clothe yourselves with compassion, kindness, humility, gentleness and patience. (Colossians 3:12 NIV)

Many of the virtues from this verse have already been discussed, such as kindness, gentleness, patience, and love. So instead of walking through this verse, I will discuss one virtue from this list (humility), and then I will discuss two additional virtues that I believe should be part of the life of any Christian that wants to pursue modesty. Although most of these have been mentioned throughout our discussion of good virtues, their connection to modesty is often overlooked. While some of these character traits may seem like surprising choices for this list, they will hopefully help fill in some of the gaps in our understanding of biblical modesty and help us discover the freedom that is found in embracing our identity in Jesus.

HUMILITY

By now, you might be thinking "Haven't we already talked about this humility stuff? Why do we need to keep bringing it up?" It's true that we have already talked some about humility, but it's so important to our discussion that it's worth diving in a little deeper. In fact, I would even argue that in this case, the words "modesty" and "humility" are synonyms. There are even two different verses that talk about being clothed in humility (Colossians 3:12 and 1 Peter

5:5) Just like modesty, humility is another word that is misunderstood and misused in our culture. Some of the traits that are often associated with humility are shyness, lack of confidence, and self-deprecation, which is having a "nobody loves me; everybody hates me" attitude toward life. To me, these traits have nothing to do with humility. In fact, self-deprecation is often a symptom of false humility, which is when you are proud of how humble you are and contradict yourself. When you look at it that way, it's a form of self-centeredness or arrogance. You are still focused on yourself when you adopt this mindset. In many ways, that type of vanity is almost more repelling than the arrogant version of it.

Let me give another example from *Beauty and the Beast* to illustrate my point. Most people would agree that Gaston is as vain as a peacock. He is so absorbed with himself, his physical appearance, and his own self-interest, a woman like Belle finds him repulsive. Labeling Gaston as arrogant and self-absorbed is a no-brainer, but even the biggest fans of the film will miss another main character who is just as vain as Gaston: Beast. With his portrayal in the 2017 live-action film, this idea makes a little more sense. The prince was quite vain in his human state until the enchantress cursed him and his household. However, the prince is not who I'm talking about. Beast is not a character that most people would associate with vanity, but the truth is that he was just as absorbed in his physical appearance as Gaston was. He was so upset about how hideous and ugly he was, he had no room in his heart to care for the needs of others. In many ways, that attitude was just as repulsive to Belle as Gaston, until Belle learns how to see past his self-centeredness and external appearance.

In this way, self-deprecation is just as repelling as the arrogant form of vanity and still does not reflect a heart that wants to honor the Lord. A humble heart isn't one that talks down about itself all the time or thinks that they are insignificant. A humble heart is one that is so concerned with the needs of others and honoring the Lord, it doesn't think that much about itself. Not to say that humble people neglect their basic needs, but instead, they choose to put the energy that would have spent dwelling on themselves or their problems and focus on the needs of others. I believe this ideal is the heart of biblical modesty. We should have our hearts so focused on doing for others and honoring the Lord, we don't have time to be dwelling on ourselves in vain or self-deprecating ways. We need to find a way to be somewhere in the middle, not self-centered but also not self-hating. This balance should be reflected in the way that we dress, not being overdressed but not being underdressed either.

Remember the illustration I gave earlier about wearing Belle's yellow dress to church? Well, let's imagine the opposite of this situation. This time, imagine I chose to show up to church in leopard print PJs with matching slippers, looking like I had just rolled out of bed. In truth the result would be almost identical to the first: it would be just as much of a distraction to those trying to worship God than being overdressed. That's why we have to find a balance between overdressed and underdressed, between being too humble and too confident. That's where you find the heart of modesty.

GRACE (FORGIVENESS)

This may seem like a surprising choice as a virtue of a modest life, but I think that there is a lot of confusion about what grace is in the first place. I have come to believe that a gracious spirit is one of the most important traits a Christian can have, but the heart of this topic is a subject that a lot of people tend to avoid: forgiveness. We don't like to think about forgiving those who have hurt us. If you have been deeply wounded by anyone, forgiveness is really hard, but living in a prison of bitterness where you refuse to forgive is even harder. We often think that by holding onto our anger and bitterness, we are punishing our offenders, when in reality we are only punishing ourselves by avoiding reconciliation and separating ourselves from God.

One of the major keys to living a lifestyle of modesty is learning how to lay all of our burdens at the feet of Jesus and therefore letting go of all the chains of our past mistakes. This includes choosing to forgive anyone who has ever hurt you. You might be thinking, "But you have no idea what I've been through! There's no way I can forgive them!" It's true that I don't know your individual story, but I can tell you that I have been through my fair share of pain and heartache caused by the actions of others. I have been in your shoes, wondering if I would ever be able to forgive those who hurt me, especially when the list of offenders was pretty long. However, I eventually realized that I had some major misunderstandings about what the Bible teaches us about grace. These truths I'm going to share with you were the key to helping me live in freedom from the burden of bitterness. These are the lessons I learned:

First, I learned that grace doesn't mean you are letting the offender off the hook. After all, you are only punishing yourself when you hold onto resentment. Scripture tells us that it's God's job to avenge for us (Deuteronomy 32:35). This means that you can choose to let yourself off the hook from the burden of your anger and bitterness. There may still be consequences you both have to pay for what happened, but you have to choose to give your feelings back to the Lord, fully trusting that the Lord will either bring about conviction or fulfill justice in His time, not yours.

Secondly, I learned that forgiveness is not a feeling, but a decision. You often don't feel like forgiving your offender, but the Lord calls you to forgive them regardless of your feelings. The feelings will follow your actions with time. Most of the time when the offense is deep, healing will be a long and difficult process. Trust will take time to rebuild. There will be times when you want to revert to anger and bitterness, but the Lord will help you if you ask. When you do this, faithfully trusting the Lord through the difficult process, your feelings will follow with time. Until then, the Lord simply asks that you trust Him with the burden of your anger and bitterness so that you can find rest in Him. Learning to pursue forgiveness even when your feelings don't immediately follow will be one of the best ways to begin healing. At least it has been for me.

Lastly, and most importantly, I learned that our greatest motivation for forgiving our offenders is that grace is the heart of the gospel. Would it shock you if I said you can't forgive your offender on your own? You may think that contradicts what I just said, but bear with me here. It's true that in and of ourselves, we cannot forgive those who hurt us deeply, but the good news is that we don't have to do it on our own! Jesus has already forgiven them and forgiven you of whatever offenses happened between you (if you had any fault). What happens when we forgive someone is that we extend Christ's grace to them. We recognize that if Christ was able to forgive us for every sin we have ever committed, then we can learn how to forgive our offenders for one or two offenses, which always become much smaller when we compare them to all the sins of which we have been forgiven. By doing so, we become an instrument of Christ's grace to our offender.

This is why it is so important for us to develop a gracious spirit. Not only will it help rid us of the anger and bitterness that holds us back, but it gives us an incredible opportunity to live out the heart of the gospel, to be Jesus to the world around us. If you have any bitterness in your heart toward anyone, especially toward a fellow believer, work it out now. Don't wait. Ask the Lord to help you let it all go. Ask for His forgiveness for holding onto anger and resentment. Whenever it's possible, seek out reconciliation. Tell them that you're sorry for your bitterness and for any other part you may have had in the offense. It's not always possible or appropriate in certain situations, but when we can, it allows us to live out the gospel. If you can't see that person specifically, seek out someone they were close to. Saying the words, "I forgive you" to your offender can be very therapeutic. Having the humility to admit when you are wrong and choosing to instead do what is right is a call on every Christian's life and is part of the heart of living out biblical modesty.

GRATITUDE

"Thank you" is a phrase that is often unappreciated in our culture. We often say it without thinking about it or meaning what we say. We complain about every little thing and get overwhelmed when we face difficult circumstances. This seems to be especially true for Christians, and we get frustrated when we are told that we are to "give thanks in all circumstances," (1 Thessalonians 5:18 NIV) because we often don't know where to start. We want the joy found in an abundant life in Christ, but we are unsure how to pursue it and maintain it.

Through a lot of difficult circumstances in my life, I have learned that one of the keys to helping me overcome my greatest obstacles is my ability to be grateful. It starts with being grateful for the basics: your salvation, your family, daily food, the clothes on your back, a house to live in, friends, and the list could go on. Once you start, it can become pretty hard to stop. If you are struggling with gratitude at this moment, I encourage you to put this book down and start making a physical list of anything and everything you're grateful for. When you think you're finished, then I encourage you to look at the most difficult circumstances you are currently facing and find something in those difficulties to be thankful for. I know better than anyone that this is easier said than done, but what I have found is that choosing to look at my struggles through the lens of gratitude has changed my perspective on all my circumstances. It's changed my perspective on life and has become a key to overcoming many other struggles, such as self-centeredness, anger, and anxiety.

So what does gratitude have to do with modesty? Well, if we believe Jesus died for us, then we will genuinely desire to obey the Scripture's guidelines about how we should dress, not out of obligation, but out of gratitude for what Jesus did for us. If gratitude is one of the motivating factors, then we need to adopt this mindset in all areas of our lives, not just with the topics of modesty and self-worth. It's a key to living a life of joy and peace, even in the middle of our most difficult circumstances, and it's one of the best ways to develop an attitude that brings glory to the Lord. That is something we should all be striving for.

PART 3

Making A Choice

9. Appropriate to the Occasion

Does anyone remember the reality show *What Not to Wear*? For those of you that don't remember, I will give you a basic summary: Each episode would start with a person who was nominated by friends and/or family, all of which were embarrassed by the state of the nominee's wardrobe. The show would secretly film the nominee for two weeks, catching some pretty embarrassing wardrobe moments. After two weeks, fashion experts Stacy London and Clinton Kelly would surprise the nominee by showing up somewhere with their camera crew.

After finding out how embarrassed everyone around them was by their appearance, Clinton and Stacy would offer the nominee a $5000 gift card to spend in New York City to revamp their entire wardrobe and get a makeover. The main stipulation was that they had to surrender their *entire* wardrobe to Clinton and Stacy, having everything the hosts didn't like thrown away, which was often everything they had. They were also forced to shop by Clinton's and Stacy's rules, often getting called out for breaking them. They would also face embarrassment when they had their wardrobe and even their undergarments criticized on national television. After a week in New York, the nominee would return home and have a big party to reveal their transformation, where everyone was so excited that this person finally looked socially acceptable.

Although there were elements of the show that I liked, I have a lot of problems with the faulty premise of this show. I admit that almost all of the people that made it on the show did need a major wardrobe overhaul. Much of what these people were wearing was unflattering, tacky, or just plain awkward. I guess it just bothered me that their family and friends were so embarrassed by their appearance that they nominated them to be humiliated on national television. Maybe one of the reasons it bothered me is that some people made jokes about nominating me when I was a teenager, just because I didn't meet their expectations about the way I should dress. It illustrates the prevailing mindset in our culture that taking pride in your appearance is necessary to make it anywhere in this world.

When a lot of Christian young women think about dressing modestly, many picture scenes like the show *What Not to Wear*. Except instead of Clinton and Stacy, you would either have your parents or leaders in your church come into your bedroom to criticize and throw away most of your wardrobe. This would cause the opposite effect of the show: they would go from fashion fabulous to fashion flop, being forced to wear clothes that are unflattering or out of style.

This perspective on modesty is problematic, to say the least. When we only address the physical symptoms of this problem, the way that we present ourselves on the outside, we will never be able to improve the underlying cause of the problem: the attitude of our heart. We've already talked about how modesty isn't a list of rules we have to keep to be good enough. Instead, modesty is willfully choosing not to draw inappropriate or unnecessary attention to yourself so that you can bring glory to God with the way you live your life.

This is the chapter where I plan to start giving modesty tips. However, I do not plan on turning this chapter into the Christian version of *What Not to Wear* as I just described. Instead, I want to give you practical guidelines based on Scripture to help you determine if your outfit is "appropriate to the occasion." I recommend you ask yourself these five questions when you get dressed in the morning:

1. AM I FOLLOWING ANY RULES ABOUT WHAT I SHOULD WEAR?

If you have been given any guidelines about how you should dress (like at school or a job), then you need to follow those rules as closely as possible. It doesn't matter if you don't like them or disagree with them. If you are in any sort of institution, you agreed to submit to their rules. Something that constantly frustrated me during my time in Christian college was when students were mad about the rules they had to follow, acting like the school was holding them back from a better life. If they had asked me, I would have reminded them that when they first became a student, they signed a student covenant that affirmed that we would submit to the rules of the school.

As Christians, we believe that God has granted every government and institution its authority, for "there is no authority except that which God has established (Romans 13:1 NIV)." Therefore, when you obey your school or work dress code, you are also obeying the Lord. Unless what they are asking you to wear is inappropriate or contradicts Scripture, then you need to choose to obey or find a new school or job.

2. AM I EXPOSING TOO MUCH OF ANY PART OF MY BODY?

Although I believe that modesty is not a list of rules, I still struggle to understand how many Christian women think that it is acceptable to expose parts of our bodies that were only meant to be seen by one other person besides you: your husband. If you aren't married, even if you are dating or engaged, no one should be seeing the deepest secrets of your beauty. Anytime that you do expose yourself, you are drawing the focus to yourself, not God.

Instead of *What Not to Wear*, this section will become *What Not to Expose*. Some parts of your body should never be exposed in public:

- <u>Your cleavage</u> – Breasts are extremely sexualized in American culture. This is not true all around the world, especially in cultures where the public breastfeeding of infants is common. There are even some countries where a woman can't have her head uncovered in public but can expose her breast to feed her child.[1] Does that sound crazy? That's because American culture has reduced the significance of breastfeeding and turned a part of our body that was designed by God for practical use into a method of sexualizing women.

  Although there should be exceptions made in the context of breastfeeding, I don't think that it's OK under any circumstances to use your breasts and cleavage as an accessory. Ever since the 1960s when the V neckline started to become more prevalent, necklines have been falling lower and lower. Don't buy into the lie that your cleavage is an accessory; it's a precious gift that God intended to be enjoyed by only one person, your husband.

- <u>Your backside</u> – With the rise in popularity of items such as low rise pants, belly shirts, crop tops, and super short shorts, we have been seeing a whole lot more "plumber's crack" and "cheek leak" than we used to. I've seen more than I've ever wanted to see, that's for sure. Although most people would agree that completely exposing your backside is inappropriate (and in most cases illegal), it's become acceptable to expose only the top part of it. If it's wrong to expose all of it, you shouldn't expose part of it. If whatever you are wearing results in any part of your backside being exposed, it's time to get a belt or dig through your closet for something else.

- <u>Your crotch</u> – This really should go without saying, but it, unfortunately, has to be brought up. There are no circumstances in which it is appropriate for this area of your body to be publically exposed or displayed (In fact, it's illegal!). Out of all the areas of our body to keep safe and covered, this one is by far the most important.

- <u>Your undergarments</u> – Although this is not a body part, there are still no circumstances in which any of your undergarments should be exposed because they immediately allude to what's underneath. Your bra straps are not accessories and your colorful underwear is not a fashion statement (please say no to whale tail!). Even Clinton and Stacy would agree with me on this one: exposing your undergarments is tacky.

There are other areas of our body that, although I can't make an absolute statement about how appropriate it is, I believe it's unwise to expose them publically. Exposing these areas willfully usually leads to compromise on your end, and can lead to temptation on a guy's end:

- Your back (especially your lower back)
- Your stomach/naval

91

- Your thighs (the upper 1/3 portion of your legs)
- Your hips

None of these suggestions are rules set in stone. I think there are ways to expose the shoulders in modest ways. I know some of you do not agree with me. Some of these standards need to become personal convictions, but the standards you set need to be founded on Scripture and wise counsel, not solely on your personal preferences. If when you are finished dressing you find that you are exposing any of these parts of your body, then you probably need to consider wearing something else or wearing layers underneath what you already have on.

Also, be careful of clothing that may be too big. There are times when wearing oversized clothing will draw attention to yourself or expose you. When I went through some drastic weight loss a few years ago, it was a struggle to see how much of my larger clothing I could work with and how much of it I just had to give up. Making sure you're wearing items that are properly sized will make it easier to keep everything properly covered.

3. AM I DRAWING ATTENTION TO WHAT'S UNDERNEATH MY CLOTHES?

Just because everything is covered doesn't necessarily mean that it is modest. Sometimes, it can be too tight. If your clothing is so tight that you can tell exactly what's underneath it, then it is not modest. If you know you're looking at a part of your body you shouldn't expose, then you shouldn't be drawing unnecessary attention to it while it's under your clothes either. We shouldn't see the outline of your undergarments through your shirt or your pants. Your shirt shouldn't be so tight that it makes your chest look bigger or makes it appear like you're going to bust out of your shirt (pun intended). Wearing leggings as pants isn't wise if your top isn't long enough to cover your backside and your front side. If you have to lay down on the bed to get your jeans on, then it's time to let go of the pants. If you are wearing a button-up shirt with a gap issue, consider wearing another layer underneath. Avoiding writing or designs on the seat of your pants is probably a wise move, too.

The only time that it is OK to be wearing tight clothing items is when they are meant to be support layers. The best example of this is a sports bra. A sports bra needs to be tight so that you don't draw attention to your chest when you are doing physical activities. Other items such as Spanks, biker shorts, and slimming tanks are support layers and acceptable to wear, but the key is that this tight layer is under your other clothes and that it isn't drawing attention to areas you shouldn't expose.

4. AM I ABLE TO FUNCTION IN THE CLOTHING I'M WEARING?

While I think these first few questions are important, I think this is the one that is the most often overlooked. While so many of our wardrobe choices look great at the beginning of the day when we first put them on, they often don't look as good by the end of the day. Your jeans fit great before you went to school, but by the end of the day, there's stretched out a bit and you're having to pull them up every 10 minutes. Your dress looked cute when you tried it on, but the first time you have to bend over to pick something up, you realize that the dress isn't as long in the back as you thought, so you have to avoid bending over to avoid embarrassment.

Most of us have found ourselves in these situations before. I think the main reason is that we try our clothes on like we're mannequins, even though we don't live like mannequins. You have to learn to test your outfits to see if they will work while you're living everyday life. A simple method that I devised to remember this goes with the nursery rhyme "Head, Shoulders, Knees, and Toes."

- <u>Head</u> – Reach your hands over your head and look in the mirror to see if your shirt is too short. (This is sometimes called the "Hallelujah Test".)

- <u>Shoulders</u> – Instead of touching your shoulders, cross your arms in an "X" in front of you and behind you so you can see if the shirt fits through the shoulders.

- <u>Knees</u> – Touch your knees and look back in the mirror to see if your chest is hanging out of your neckline.

- <u>Toes</u> – Especially if you are wearing a dress, skirt, or shorts, turn your backside to the mirror before you touch your toes to see the view someone else would get if you bend over in front of them. You can also check your pants this way to see if the seam is riding too far into your backside.

In addition to this, you should also sit down to see if your pants are comfortable through the seat, or how much your dress or skirt rides up (you can repeat "Knees and Toes" a second time like the song while sitting to help you remember). These are all steps you should repeat any time you try on clothes in the fitting room or when you are getting dressed for the day. It will look different for different people, but the point is that you shouldn't test your clothes standing still in front of the mirror. Be active when you try things on to see if they work in the real world. If they don't, then there's no point in wearing them.

With this in mind, I want to warn those of you who have been raised with more conservative traditions against ignoring the functionality of your clothes for the sake of modesty. I was a cheerleader in junior high and high school. Since I went to a Christian school, modesty was one of our greatest concerns when it came to choosing uniforms. Our school dress code required that skirts had to be to our knees. Before my first year of cheerleading, the squad wore skirts of that length, but right before I joined the squad, some research came to light that showed that wearing skirts of that length while cheering could be dangerous. This was because some cheerleaders had actually hurt or even broken their fingers when they got caught in their skirts, especially when the skirts were pleaded. For the skirts to be safe, they needed to be shorter than our fingertips so they wouldn't get caught, but this was far too short to be acceptable for our dress code.

After discovering this, our coach decided that instead of choosing between modesty and safety, we would go a completely different route: we would wear pants instead of skirts. There's no denying that we stood out from all the other squads. It would take a few tries to get a uniform design that worked well with our pants, but when we finally got it right we began to get a lot of compliments on our uniforms. We even saw one or two other squads in our division that started wearing pants before I graduated.

Don't assume that dysfunctional clothes are OK because they cover more. If you are dressed so "modestly" that you can't live everyday life in your clothes, you will probably be drawing attention to yourself, which will make your clothing immodest by default. If you find yourself struggling with this, bring it before the Lord. Ask Him to reveal to you how to remain modest while still wearing clothes that function with your needs. I think you will find that there is more freedom than you realize in a lifestyle of modesty if you let go of traditions and instead hold onto the truth of God's Word.

5. Am I able to take any available opportunity to honor the Lord Today?

So far, we've talked about glorifying the Lord with our clothing, but we've not necessarily talked about what it looks like to put this into practice. While it's important to follow any given rules, keep it covered, keep it a little loose, and make sure it's functional, the reason we do any of this is so we can take the attention that would have been focused on us and instead bring glory to the God we profess to worship. How we dress each day will often determine how prepared we are to meet the needs of those around us and our ability to bring glory to God.

I wear my tennis shoes almost everywhere. This is in part due to a problem I have with my arches, but the other reason is that I feel tennis shoes are the most useful of all my pairs of shoes. Although I do wear flats with dresses and skirts, I'm always worried when I do that something could happen and I won't be wearing the right shoes if I have to walk. My tennis shoes are my most versatile pair of shoes when I need to get things done. I wear them to work and I wear them to play. When I switched from white to black tennis shoes a few years ago, I wore them even more, because they blended with my wardrobe more naturally. I believe that wearing these shoes best equips me to serve others when the opportunity presences itself.

If we are dressed just right for every occasion, we will be better prepared to take any and every opportunity available to honor the Lord by serving others. So if you are ready to take up the call, start looking for opportunities to serve. They are all around you. From church to school to work to your own backyard, opportunities will meet you where you are, if you open your heart to honor the Lord with your life and your wardrobe.

10. Real Questions about Modern Modesty

As we have been talking about the heart of modesty, we have been sticking mostly with either debunking lies or the facts that Scripture declares as the truth about modesty and our identity. By now, some of you may have some questions about how these concepts work in the world we live in today. While the churches in Paul's letter lived in the first century, we live in the twenty-first century. Trying to apply biblical truth in our modern context can sometimes be much easier said than done. Figuring out where to start can be even harder, so the next two chapters of this book will be devoted to answering questions about how to apply these truths in our world today. Many of these questions have been asked by girls in the Bible studies I've taught over the years. A few are simply topics that need to be discussed, but all of them should help you see how to apply what we have learned so far to what's in your closet now. Let's dive right in:

What about makeup, hairdos, and accessories? Didn't Paul and Peter tell us we can't wear them?

Do you remember when Paul said in 1 Timothy that women should adorn themselves? The key is to learn how to adorn ourselves *appropriately*. I believe this gives us the freedom to do what we want with makeup, hair, and accessories. We just have to learn how to figure out what is appropriate for each situation.

Hairdos of the first century were much different than today. Most middle class or lower class women probably left their hair down under their head coverings. Only the upper class women would have worn their hair in braids or up-dos, and the problem with these women showing up to church with these hairstyles was that they were using them to elevate their social status. I don't think we have the same problem today. Hairdos such as braids, buns, pony/pigtails, curls, and straightened hair are incredibly commonplace, so wearing them doesn't attract the same kind of attention as it did in the first century. Unless you are wearing your prom hairdo to school to get attention, you've probably OK to do what you want with your hair within reason. Just make sure that you are obeying any given rules about hairstyles, that you don't draw unnecessary attention with your hairstyles, and that you choose to honor the femininity that God has given you if you choose to go with a shorter length of hair. Then you should be in good shape.

Makeup, as women wear it today, is much different than what women of the first century would have worn. In that society, most of the women who wore makeup were either upper class women or prostitutes. That's not the case today. Cosmetics are much more affordable than they used to be and much more commonplace. While this could be a good thing, I believe that the use of makeup has perhaps become a little too commonplace. There are too many women in our culture that won't let anyone see them without their makeup on. The way their face looks with makeup has become the standard of their public appearance. They feel incomplete without it. This should not be. I feel very strongly that my appearance with makeup should be the exception, not the standard, of my public appearance. I understand wearing makeup being a standard at work, especially if you work in an office setting. I also understand using it for formal or casual occasions. But if you feel like you can't leave the house without plastering makeup on your face, you need to ask the Lord to give you wisdom about how to allow the beauty He's given you to shine through naturally. [If you want to take up this challenge, check out the first appendix of this book to learn more about doing a vanity fast.]

Accessories are also different than they were in the first century because they are much more commonplace. You can buy them for much less of someone's average wage than they did in the first century. You have to determine for yourself if any of your necklaces, earrings, bracelets, shoes, scarves, purses, or other accessories are too much for any given situation. It starts with just asking the question, "Does wearing this draw too much attention to myself?"

DOESN'T 1 CORINTHIANS 11:5-6 TELL US THAT WOMEN CAN'T PRAY WITHOUT THEIR HEADS COVERED? DOES THAT MEAN I AM REQUIRED TO WEAR A HEAD COVERING TO CHURCH?

No, I do not believe women are required to cover their heads today. There are some important things we have to understand when looking at this passage. First, this practice was meant to be mostly within the context of those participating in prophesying as part of corporate worship, which is something that doesn't happen in modern church services. Covering their heads was meant to be part of a woman's reverence, just as it was part of a man's reverence to keep his head uncovered. However, we live in a day and age where not only is prophesying not a part of corporate worship, but the tradition of head covering is not commonly practiced, either in the church or within most cultures at large. I've seen some American women that take the head covering instructions of Paul quite literally and wear them daily in public. I don't agree with this interpretation. Because it's no longer a standard cultural practice, head coverings can become a distraction and a means to draw attention to yourself. If it becomes a distraction to anyone, then it's not modest in the first place. Unless you live in a country or are working within a cultural context where head covering is commonly practiced, I don't think this practice is useful or practical for women to do today.

Is it OK for Women to wear pants?

Yes, I believe that it's acceptable for women to wear pants. While it's true that women back in the first century did not wear pants, men didn't either! Assuming that because the women of the Bible had to wear tunics that we have to wear skirts is kind of strange logic, because that would mean that men would also still be wearing skirts!

There was a time when it was acceptable for men to wear pants or breeches, but it was considered inappropriate for a woman to do the same. We no longer live in that time. We live in a day and age where it is considered normal and socially acceptable for both men and women to wear pants. This means that in most settings, it would not be considered a distraction for women to wear them. I believe this gives us the freedom to use the Scriptures to discern which pants are appropriate to wear. My main stipulations are that my pants need to avoid looking overtly masculine and that they need to avoid being too tight. Other than that, I believe that I can choose to wear whatever pants I want within reason. If you choose to wear only skirts, that's your decision, but I caution you to avoid letting this conviction become a distraction to those around you by sacrificing the functionality of your outfit or choosing to wear a skirt in an inappropriate setting. If it becomes a distraction to anyone, then it wasn't modest in the first place.

Does a Christian girl have to dress up for church? What is appropriate to wear to a church service?

No, I do not believe that women are required to dress up for church. The Bible doesn't tell us that we are required to wear dresses, skirts, or formal clothes. What it does tell us is that we should not allow anything about our outward appearance to become a distraction for anyone worshipping the Lord. Some churches uphold traditions that look down on those who don't dress up. In that context, refusing to dress up may prove to be a distraction, but outside of this context, I don't think any of us are required to wear formal clothes to church every week.

I grew up as a pastor's kid, so before going to college out of state, I only remember wearing pants to a church service twice in the 18 years of my life. I always wore a dress or a skirt, not out of obligation from tradition, but because my family wanted to set an example by dressing well. When I was in college and started going to a church near my college town, I remember feeling strange the first time I wore dress pants on a Sunday. I knew there was nothing wrong with it; I just wasn't used to it. My perspective has changed on this over the years since my dad is no longer in ministry. Now, I don't feel strange wearing jeans to a church service, as long as that church's traditions make it acceptable for me to do so. What matters the most is that you show up to church, not what you wear. Whether you dress up or dress down, just remember to never allow your appearance to become a distraction for worshipping the Lord.

SHOULD MODESTY STANDARDS LOOK DIFFERENT FOR MARRIED WOMEN THAN THEY DO FOR SINGLE WOMEN?

No, I don't think modesty standards should change once you get married. The way that a married woman practices them will look different from how single women practice them, but I don't think the principles change. One of the goals of modesty should be to save your beauty for your husband. Just because you get married and you have shared that beauty with him, it doesn't mean you're off the hook. I think it makes the stakes higher for you to guard your secret so that no one tries to steal it from you or your husband. There will be a context where you can wear more revealing things in the privacy of your marriage, but the standard of what you wear in public shouldn't change just because you say "I do."

While we're on the subject of marriage, I want to warn any single girls reading this against believing the lie that marriage is the end goal of dressing modestly or pursuing purity. At the time I am writing this, I am 29 years old and single. I've never been on a real date. For the record, although I still wish to be married someday, I am doing my best to choose contentment in this season of life. This was much harder to do when I fell into one of the most common lies of the purity movement that was popular in my teen years: if you pursue purity and don't have sex before marriage, God will give you a husband. Now I realize that marriage is not promised to any of us in the Scriptures. Many of us that do get married won't get married in the timeframe we imagine for ourselves. What He does promise is that if we accept the gift of His salvation, we will never be alone. I want to encourage you as a fellow single girl, don't dress modestly in hopes that it will earn you a husband. Dress modestly so that you will be in the best position to honor the Lord and live this season of your life to the fullest.

SHOULDN'T GUYS DRESS MODESTLY TOO?

Absolutely. I remember the first time I heard this question asked. When I was teaching my first Bible study, I invited the dads of the girls to join us one night so that the girls could hear a man's/father's perspective on modesty. After I asked the dads a few questions, I opened up the floor for the girls to ask anything they wanted. They were feeling pretty shy about it. They were kind of huddled together, trying to figure out what they were going to ask. When I came over to them, I managed to figure out the one question they were hesitant to ask: why do girls have to dress modestly, but guys don't? I was surprised that these young girls came up with such a profound question. Frankly, so were their dads. That conversation helped me realize that there is a double standard when it comes to men and modesty. Many men will work out just so they can flaunt their bodies and seduce women. As much as it bothers me to see women that let their underwear hang out the back of their pants, it's even worse with guys (Seriously, has anyone heard of this thing called a belt?).

In short, yes, I believe that men should learn to dress modestly to divert the attention off of themselves and back to God. As much as they bear responsibility for controlling what their minds choose to dwell on, they also need to learn to have humility in their physical presentation so they won't set up young women to be in the same position. Although the Scriptures about modesty aren't necessarily addressed to them, there are plenty of verses about humility and other virtues from which they can apply these concepts to their lives. Just remember that men have the same responsibilities as women do, avoiding creating temptation and avoiding falling into temptation.

[Note: If your dad, brother, or guy friend is interested in gaining some perspective on this topic, have them read Appendix 2 of this book]

SHOULD MY HEIGHT AND BODY TYPE BE A FACTOR WHEN I'M EVALUATING THE MODESTY OF MY CLOTHES?

Absolutely. One of the reasons why many dress codes are frustrating to me is because they try to make rules that are "one size fits all." In truth, there's no such thing as one size fits all. One of the beautiful parts of the way God designed humanity is that there is so much diversity in the way each one of our bodies is designed. This does play a factor in the modesty of your clothing choices. Some skirts that are modest on the girl who's only 5 ½ ft. would not be modest on the girl who's 6 ft. with long legs. Girls with a more slender frame might be able to pull off skinny jeans while the curvy girl can't because it would be too tight around her hips. A button-up blouse that works on a girl with narrow shoulders may not work on a girl who has broad shoulders. It's important to learn what works with your body type so you don't run into these problems. If you are unsure, ask your mom, sister, or close friend to help you. Otherwise, you run the risk of drawing attention to yourself with immodest or unflattering clothes.

WHAT IF I HAVE CLOTHING THAT ISN'T MODEST, BUT I DON'T WANT TO GIVE IT UP?

If you have used the questions we discussed in the last chapter and discovered that some of your favorite clothing doesn't pass, you may be struggling to part with them. Whether it be from memories made in these clothes or liking how we look in them, we all get attracted to our clothing. I know that I have struggled to give up some of my clothes after I realized it was too small on me (or too big after I lost weight). If you are struggling with this, bring it before the Lord. Ask Him to change your heart to be willing to give up the clothing you love so that He can become a higher priority in your life. It will be hard, especially if you are in love with fashion, but the Lord will bless your obedience if you trust Him to guide you.

As far as what you should do with the clothes, I have a few suggestions: 1. Check to make sure there isn't a way to rework your clothing with layers. Laying tank tops (which we will talk about with the next question) can fix a lot of issues of exposing too much. 2. Donate or give away the clothes that are too small or too big. If the only issue is that they aren't the right size for you, then you can choose to bless someone else. 3. Find a way to repurpose old clothes. Make things like t-shirts quilts or artwork with your old clothes. There are plenty of ideas on Pinterest or other places online. 4. If you know that you nor anyone else could ever wear this item modestly, then you just need to throw it away. Don't give it to someone else knowing that it could become a problem for them later. If you know it would cause someone to sin, throw it out (Matthew 5:29-30).

DO YOU HAVE ANY "MODESTY MUST-HAVES" THAT YOU RECOMMEND TO HELP ME DRESS MODESTLY BUT FASHIONABLE?

Yes, I do! Here's my top ten list:

1. <u>Layering Tank Tops</u> – The key to fixing many of the issues with clothes off the rack is tank tops that can be layered under your shirts and/or tucked into your pants. The main type I look for is spaghetti-strapped tanks, with straps that can be adjusted the full length of the strap. The best way to get the most coverage for your chest is to pull the straps all the way forward so that the clips are resting in front of your shoulders. Tucking the tank into your pants or skirt will ensure that the tank stays in place. Make sure to test the coverage of the tank by touching your knees in front of the mirror. Do your diligence to track some down and you will find them in multiple colors so that you will always have a modesty solution on hand.

2. <u>Slips</u> – Slips are an extra layer to wear under skirts and dresses, usually made out of silky or satin-like materials with an elastic band. It ensures that if the material of your skirt is sheer, no one will be able to see through it. You will also find that slips will make your skirts and dresses more comfortable by providing an extra layer. They come in a variety of lengths and colors. They are much harder to find in store than they used to be, but many major retailers still carry them online.

3. <u>Bra Strap Clips</u> – These handy plastic clips are used to help conceal your bra straps under certain tops by pulling them into a racerback style. Another thing these clips can be used for is spaghetti-strap layering tanks. If you want to wear a tank top with a lower neck, but don't

want the straps of the layering tank to be hanging out, this could be your solution.

4. Neutral Colored Underwear/Bras – If you find yourself wearing sheer clothing and you worry that your undergarments will show through, then you need to make sure that you have at least a few pairs of beige/light-colored underwear and a few beige bras. I know that bright colored bras and underwear are fun, but no one else needs to see them, especially if you aren't married. You don't have to wear them exclusively, but making sure that you have them available in case you need them is important. While we're on the subject, I think every young woman should have at least one sports bra and one strapless bra, just in case they need one. You don't want to find yourself in a situation where you need one, but don't have one.

5. Belts – I think both men and women need to learn the importance of wearing belts. Their purpose is to keep your pants up! This is not a problem for those that are used to wearing business or formal attire. Where it's usually a problem is casual or comfortable attire, especially jeans or shorts. If you don't already, you should wear a belt with all of your jeans or shorts that have belt loops. It will usually solve the problem of showing your underwear or "plumber's crack" instantly.

6. Spanks and Biker Shorts – Spanks are slimming shorts that you wear under skirts or dresses. Aside from smoothing out your stomach, Spanks also provide a layer between your slip and your underwear if either your skirt falls down or your dress blows up. Spanks brand, however, is expensive. If you can't afford that brand, there are usually cheaper alternatives at local retail stores. Biker shorts can be a good substitute, depending on the material

of the dress/skirt. It's important to have that extra layer under your skirt if something goes wrong.

7. Slimming Tanks – Just like with Spanks, slimming tanks will help smooth out your stomach and prevent anything underneath from being seen. They also provide an extra layer, especially in the winter months. These are available at many local retailers.

8. Leggings – Although there should be caution used with the length of tops or skirts worn with them (which we will talk about in the next chapter), leggings can help solve some issues with the length of dresses or skirts. They are also great to have on hand in the winter as an extra layer to wear under other clothes.

9. Guys' T-Shirts, Shorts, and Tanks – I am so grateful that they don't make belly shirts, crop tops, or booty shorts for guys! This is something that we can use to our advantage. I recommend getting some solid color t-shirts with a regular neckline from the guy's department if you want to layer them underneath other shirts. Guys tanks (which are sometimes referred to as "wife beaters") also have a higher neckline and longer length than most women's tanks. Some men's athletic shorts and cargo style shorts can work for girls too if they aren't too masculine (just remember that men's pants are sized by waist measurements). Sometimes, you just have to get creative.

10. Infinity Fashion Scarfs – Not only can these be used to help cover your chest (although it probably shouldn't be the only layer covering your cleavage in case you need to take it off), I think they are a good way to divert attention away from your chest and up to your face. This is not meant to be vain, but if someone is going to notice me, I want them looking at my face, not the rest of my body.

11. Real Questions about What We Should Wear

In the last chapter, we answered a few practical questions about how modesty works in our world today. In this chapter, we are answering questions about clothing items that many Christian girls wonder if they should wear at all or if they are modest alternatives to what most women wear. I want to remind you that although I am sharing my opinions here, I have tried my hardest to allow my opinions on these matters to be shaped by the truth of Scripture. If you find yourself resistant to any of the things I'm saying here, make sure to check your heart to see if this resistance is from pride because you don't want to change, or from a conviction that what I'm saying is Scripturally incorrect. If it's pride, then you need to ask the Lord to help you get over your pride so you can do what He's asking of you. If it's a conviction, check to make sure you are reading that Scripture correctly, and if you are, stand by it. Please don't let your ability to obey the Lord be hindered by your desire to fit in or to stay in your comfort zone. There is so much more to life than seeking the approval of others or our personal comfort.

Should a Christian girl wear a bikini?

Personally, I don't think that Christian women should wear bikinis. It's my opinion that they are unwise to wear, especially in the context of public swimming. They do not pass most of the questions we asked in chapter nine and can have consequences for those that see you wearing them. To understand what I mean, I encourage you to go look up the YouTube video, "The Evolution of the Swimsuit" by Jessica Rey. This video not only explains the history of this type of swimsuit but also the negative impact it has on the minds of men when you wear one.[1]

If you still aren't sure, let me ask a straightforward question: would you be comfortable walking around publically in your underwear? If you wouldn't be comfortable in your underwear in public, then why would you be comfortable in a bikini in public? While wearing one, many of the secrets of your beauty, the ones that are meant to be for your husband only, are put on display for everyone to see. I often describe bikinis as water-proof underwear when I'm teaching young girls, because it paints an honest picture. The reasons "but everyone else is wearing them" or "but it's what I'm used to wearing" are not good enough reasons to continue to wear them, because Christians are called to avoid conforming to the patterns of this world (Romans 12:2).

Please understand that I am not judging you if bikinis have been your swimsuit of choice, but I believe there's something better for you than this cultural trend. If you know that the Lord is calling you to give up your bikini, ask the Lord to help you. He will give you the strength to do it if you ask.

IF I CAN'T WEAR A BIKINI, THEN WHAT SHOULD I WEAR TO THE POOL?

Because bikinis are the most popular type of swimsuit, other styles are much harder to find. Even longer two-piece suits (tankinis) and many one-piece swimsuits don't cover certain parts of our body sufficiently. However, I've seen some modest alternatives to swimwear that are so long (like knee-length swim-dresses), they aren't functional and could be dangerous. So I will give you two alternatives that cover the important areas of the body while being cute and functional. Those of you that are used to wearing bikinis will probably struggle with wearing this much to the pool, but I encourage you to do your best to honor the Lord with your swimwear, even if it isn't easy.

The first option (which I give credit to sisters Kristen Clark and Bethany Beal from Girl Defined Ministries for this idea) is to wear surf shirts (rash guards) or quick dry athletic shirts with board shorts, wearing a regular swimsuit underneath it.[2] I must admit when I first heard about this concept, I was not fond of it. After all, you're buying at least three swimwear pieces, which can be expensive. However, I started to realize that this can be a viable option. If you have a swimsuit that doesn't quite work, adding these accessories could be an option to help your swimsuit to be modest and functional.

The second option is what I have done for swimwear since I was a teenager. First, I find a one-piece swimsuit with a high neckline. This often takes quite a bit of hunting, but it can be done with time and patience. These are the swimsuits that are usually designed for athletic swimmers. They have to keep the chest covered and their torso secure so that nothing will slow down their speed. Although some would consider them tight, I think it's necessarily secure and functional for what you do in the water, like a dancer wearing a leotard so that extra fabric doesn't get in the way of their dancing. If you look in the right places, you will usually find something that is in bright, fun colors. (Just don't forget "Head, Shoulders, Knees, and Toes" when trying them on.) In addition to the swimsuit, I also wear a pair of swim shorts. This is because I don't like the attention that is drawn to my crotch or my bikini line with the swimsuits off the rack. The shorts are usually easy to find in a variety of lengths and colors to match your suit. I recommend that they not be any shorter than mid-thigh, but you can go as long as knee-length if you choose board shorts. Some of them will even have extra swim bottoms built into them for an extra layer.

Both of these are modest alternatives to modern swimwear. If you going to take on the challenge of living a lifestyle of modesty, I encourage you to allow God's Word to impact the way you dress both on land and in the water.

What should Christian girls wear during the summer when it's hot?

My mom has pointed out to me that it's better to be cold than hot. This is because when you're cold, you can put on as many layers as you need to get warm, but when you are hot, there is only so much you can appropriately take off and you will probably still be hot. Being modest during the summer can be difficult and frustrating. If you live in a state or country where the climate is generally humid, then it can be especially difficult to find enough modest clothes that won't cause you to break into a sweat. We've already discussed appropriate bathing suits, as well as avoiding things that are too short or too low cut, but I have two quick recommendations when it comes to finding clothes for hot or humid days.

First, look for a style of shorts called Bermuda shorts. They usually are cuffed at the bottom and come to the knees or just above the knee. Fortunately, this style of shorts has become more popular over the last several years, so they are becoming easier to find. They may be longer than some of you are used to, but they will cover the right areas. Just make sure they aren't too tight through the seat.

Second, be open to wearing layers during the summer when necessary. Especially if you are wearing tank tops or lighter fabrics, you still need to make sure everything is covered, especially your chest. Wearing less may seem more comfortable in the moment, but it opens you up to compromise and becomes a distraction to those around you, which is exactly what we should be trying to avoid.

Are leggings OK to wear as pants?

If you are wearing a shirt, dress, or tunic that is shorter than about your mid-thigh, then no, leggings are not an appropriate substitute for pants. Wearing leggings as pants tends to draw unnecessary attention to your backside and your crotch because they are very tight (please say no to camel toe!). If you do wear them, I encourage you to check that your front side and backside are covered by your top, especially when you bend over or sit down. Otherwise, consider wearing them like you would wear tights, viewing them as a secondary layer rather than as a primary article of clothing.

What should Christian girls wear for sports or physical activities?

Although I am the least athletic girl you'll ever meet, I have some very strong opinions when it comes to what's appropriate to wear for workouts and physical activities. Unfortunately, working out publically has become one of the ultimate ways to flaunt your body and bring all the attention to yourself. In truth, most trendy workout clothing just doesn't fit with a lifestyle of modesty, especially styles like wearing just your sports bra as a top, wearing just leggings as pants, tight yoga pants, Spandex-type shirts, Spandex shorts, and super short running shorts. All of these are designed to attract attention to your

114

body that should be focused on the God you are worshipping. Let me give you a few tips:

First, keep your sports bra hidden. Although it's a huge trend to show them off, it doesn't honor the Lord to show off your stomach and naval, or to wear a loose shirt to invite everyone to imagine what's underneath. Keep your undergarments hidden under your clothes. Second, stick to shorts that are about knee length. One of the most popular styles at this length is basketball shorts. They are super comfortable, cover everything, and they are now making them in female styles. I love to wear them, even though I don't usually work out! It's wise to avoid athletic shorts that are really short, especially running shorts. Third, stick to sleeved t-shirts or sleeveless athletic shirts with higher necklines. Most of the other popular options, like loose and low tank tops, just reveal too much. Lastly, either throw out tight clothes or consider layering them. My friend who does yoga recommended that those who do similar exercises consider layering a pair of shorts over yoga pants or leggings to make them more modest.

WHAT SHOULD A CHRISTIAN GIRL WEAR TO PROM OR A FORMAL EVENT?

Prom is often considered the highlight of a teenager's high school experience, but one of the hardest parts about prom for Christian girls is figuring out what to wear. While it's a day where it's OK to dress up, it's also a day when many immodest fashions become the standard. While we still need to be careful about revealing too much, we also don't want to draw too much attention by wearing extremely outdated dresses just because they cover more. I believe there are ways to find dresses that are modest and fashionable. Here are a couple of tips:

115

First, remember that principles about modesty still apply to prom dresses. Just because all your friends are picking dresses that are short and/or revealing doesn't mean that you should. Secondly, be prepared to hunt. Many of the dresses I found in high school were from bigger retail stores. My sisters had more success looking in small local bridal stores, which also gave them personalized service. Depending on your budget, you can find some really cute dresses if you know where to look. Third, test the dress out. When you are in the fitting room, see if you can sit well in the dress. Do the Head, Shoulders, Knees, and Toes test. If you think you are going to be tugging on the dress to keep it up or that you are worried about bending over because the dress will flip up in the back, then it's probably not a good choice. Don't settle until you know you will comfortable living in that dress for a few hours on prom night.

Fourth, make plans to get the dress altered. This is something that a lot of girls miss. One of the best ways to ensure that your dress fits well is planning to get your dress tailored, especially around your chest. There is a difference between something fitted and something tight. Fitted will appropriately complement your body, while tight will draw too much attention to your body or what's underneath your clothes. If you're going to wear a beautiful dress, you might as well do it right. Ask your mom to help you find connections to someone local who can do alterations for you. They may even be able to add modesty panels to the front or back of the dress to cover areas that are too revealing. If you happen to go to a local bridal shop, they would probably do alterations for you as part of a package. If you follow these steps, you will hopefully find something that will fit you well and is totally modest.

What should a Christian girl wear for Halloween or costume parties?

The costumes that the Halloween industry sells for adults and teens are becoming more and more risqué, but at the same time, the costumes the children wear and the candy seem pretty harmless. Halloween is marketed in such a way that it encourages you to either wear a sexy adult costume or a costume that glorifies symbols of death and fear. Whether you are dressing up to pass out candy or you're going to a party, here's a couple of principles to help you determine which costumes you can wear:

First, the principles of modesty still apply to costumes. Sexy costumes that are meant to draw attention to your body are inappropriate and always will be, not to mention that it would be super cold to wear outside if the temperature drops. Second, if you choose to be a character, you need to make sure that character is not dishonoring to the Lord. I'm not saying that you can only be Christian characters (I've been several Disney characters or superheroes over the years), but choosing to dress up like a symbol of death and fear is dishonoring to the Lord because Jesus defeated death and His love drives out fear. We shouldn't be making that into a joke. Practically any symbol of Halloween in some way, shape, or form mocks what Jesus did for us on the cross and we should think twice before choosing to honor it. Lastly, make sure your costume is functional. Aside from testing your outfit, you also need to keep an eye on the weather if you are going to be outside. If you are, you may need to get creative with layers under your costume. Although it may not look exactly like you envisioned it, it will give you the ability to help others if they need it. That should always be part of living a modest life.

12. Nurturing the Seed

As you have been reading this book, I hope that a seed has been planted in your heart, a seed of a desire to honor God with a lifestyle of humility reflected through your wardrobe. However, this can be easier said than done since our world does not value modesty like it once did.

Back in the early 1900s, women used to wear bathing costumes when they would go to the beach: bloomers to a woman's knees, and long tunic blouses that were short-sleeved. They would change out of their regular clothes in "bathing machines," small huts that would be wheeled into the water. Public swimming during this time was usually segregated because even though their costumes were extremely modest by today's standards, they were not considered appropriate attire to be seen in public.[1] When the length of women's swimwear did get shorter about 15 years later, officials at the beaches began to measure the length of women's bathing suits to make sure they didn't violate their standards. I even found a post online that had photos of two women being arrested in Chicago in 1922 for wearing one-piece swimsuits![2]

It's hard to believe that American culture could go from arresting women with one-piece swimsuits to accepting the bikini as the standard for swimwear only 40 years later, but that's the world we live in. If you allow yourself to be swayed by their lies, you will end up buying into them and living by them. Then no one will be able to tell the difference between you and the rest of the world. If you want to get serious about living a modest life, you have to nurture the seed that has been planted in your heart.

The Sower and Modesty

One of Jesus' most popular parables is a powerful illustration of what can happen when someone hears the truth of God's Word:

"A sower went out to sow. And as he sowed, some seeds fell along the path, and the birds came and devoured them. Other seeds fell on rocky ground, where they did not have much soil, and immediately they sprang up, since they had no depth of soil, but when the sun rose they were scorched. And since they had no root, they withered away. Other seeds fell among thorns, and the thorns grew up and choked them. Other seeds fell on good soil and produced grain, some a hundredfold, some sixty, some thirty. He who has ears, let him hear." (Matthew 13:3b-9 ESV)

Something that sets this parable apart from the others is the authors of each account (Matthew, Mark, and Luke) not only offer the story, but also give us the correct interpretation. Although the crowd who first heard him did not get this explanation, his disciples did when they asked for the meaning of the parable:

"Hear then the parable of the sower: When anyone hears the word of the kingdom and does not understand it, the evil one comes and snatches away what has been sown in his heart. This is what was sown along the path. As for what was sown on rocky ground, this is the one who hears the word and immediately receives it with joy, yet he has no root in himself, but endures for a while, and when tribulation or persecution arises on account of the word, immediately he falls away. As for what was sown among thorns, this is the one who hears the word, but the cares of the world and the deceitfulness of riches choke the word, and it proves unfruitful. As for what

119

was sown on good soil, this is the one who hears the word and understands it. He indeed bears fruit and yields, in one case a hundredfold, in another sixty, and in another thirty." (Matthew 13:18-23 ESV)

I think it's incredible to have the correct interpretation alongside this parable, for many scholars have struggled to accurately interpret His other parables as He meant them to be understood. We don't have to worry about this with the parable of the sower. I love that this story not only applies to evangelism (when we share the message of the gospel with unbelievers), but I believe this can also apply to seasoned Christians who have discovered new truths from the Scripture they know they need to act on.

If you have made it this far through this book, I pray that you are not the seed stolen by the birds. This is more likely to apply to your friends who may ask after you start to change the clothes you wear. When you explain it to them, they may not even be able to comprehend the idea of submitting to any modesty standards, because they have lived in a world where standards for modesty hardly exist. The seed of opportunity will probably be snatched before it ever has a chance to grow.

That's why it's important to share the heart of the gospel and the love of Christ first so that there will be at least some context for them to understand your motivation for dressing modestly. This is because from a secular standpoint, without the love of a God who created us uniquely and died for us to have a relationship with us, modesty makes no sense. That relationship has to be in place for any of these concepts to make sense to someone influenced by the world's logic on fashion.

If you aren't careful, some of you could become like the seed sown on the rocky soil. You may be excited about finding ways to implement the ideas shared in this book to your closet. It all makes sense like it never has before and you are ready to dive in. However, when you get into the heart of it and begin to face opposition for your wardrobe choices, you feel the pressure and eventually revert to wearing what you used to wear, realizing that you knew all along this would be too hard. I pray this doesn't happen to you. If you believe that these truths are based on the Word of God, I pray that the Lord gives you the strength to stand your ground when you feel pressure from the world around you. You never have to be afraid to stand up for the truth.

Some of you could also end up like the seed that fell among the thorns. In this case, you become your own worst enemy. You want to embrace the truth of God's Word when it comes to modesty, but you are worried. Worried about what your friends will think. Worried about how much time and money you will have to spend to modify your wardrobe. Worried about the clothes you love that you need to part with permanently. You start to believe the lies about your worth and value. Therefore, you stop before ever have the chance to see any fruit from these truths in your life.

If this is you, I understand how hard it can be to overcome our fears and worries. I know it's not easy to put the worries or the pressures others put on you aside, but if you know that what you have been taught is the truth, then you need to stand on it. You have to learn to lay your pride and your anxieties at the foot of the cross and trust that the Lord will sustain you through all that worries you if you act in obedience. In reality, most of what scares you will probably never come true, and what does come true will make you stronger in Christ.

I want to pray that every one of you becomes like the seed planted on good soil, but that depends on you. For the seed to take hold and produce fruit in the soil of your heart, you have to make sure your heart is ready to nurture the seed of truth that has already been planted. If you want to ensure that the seed produces fruit, here are some steps to make that happen:

Get Right with God

If there is anything in your life that is holding you back in your relationship with God, especially if it is related to modesty or purity, you need to repent before the Lord. If we believe that Jesus died for our sins then rose again so that we can live in right relationship with Him, we have to be willing to admit when we allow anything to separate us from Him. It's not about "forgiving yourself," as some people try to claim. It's about accepting His forgiveness that is already available if you ask. Getting any obstacles out of the way is necessary if you want to live a lifestyle of humility before the Lord. Psalm 51 is a great place to start:

> Create in me a pure heart, O God, and renew a steadfast spirit within me. Do not cast me from your presence or take your Holy Spirit from me. Restore to me the joy of your salvation and grant me a willing spirit, to sustain me. (Psalm 51:10-12 NIV)

Only when we ask God to renew our hearts will the seeds of truth take root. Take this step right now. If something is weighing down on you, don't wait. Ask the Lord to forgive you of your sins, fully believing that He can and He will. Especially if you know that you have struggled with using your body or your wardrobe for selfish reasons, lay it all at the feet of the One who died to free you from the burden of your worst mistakes. Ask Him to give you wisdom so that you can replace the lies about who you are with the truth of His Word. Only when these truths take root in your heart will you be ready to take the next step.

TRUST AND OBEY

The phrase "trust and obey" sounds nice, simple, and easy. There's even an old hymn with this title, but the reality is that it's one of the hardest but also most fulfilling things we will ever do with our lives. Once we have made peace with our sin before God, we have to turn away from any sinful behavior and purpose ourselves to live our lives by the principles given in Scripture. If our hearts are right before God, our obedience to His Word will not be motivated by obligation, as if we had to earn the gift of salvation that has already been given to us. Instead, it will be motivated by our gratitude for what our Savior has done for us. That's why we will offer our lives in worship to Him.

"I appeal to you therefore, brothers, by the mercies of God, to present your bodies as a living sacrifice, holy and acceptable to God, which is your spiritual worship. Do not be conformed to this world, but be transformed by the renewal of your mind, that by testing you may discern what is the will of God, what is good and acceptable and perfect." (Romans 12:1-2 ESV)

The best way to know God's will is to live our lives sacrificially for Him and refuse to give in to the ways of the world around us. When we struggle to believe that the Lord's ways are good or we are scared to follow, we need to remember Proverbs 3:5-6:

123

"Trust in the Lord with all your heart, and lean not on your own understanding; in all your ways acknowledge him, and he will make your path straight." (NIV)

If you know this to be true, you will be able to trust Him with your whole heart. When you learn to acknowledge Him, doing things His way instead of your way especially with the way you dress, the Lord will make your path clear, even amid life's uncertainty. If we lean on our own understanding, we will fall time and time again. Only leaning on the truth of His Word will keep you going in the right direction, and that's one of the best ways to honor the Lord with the way you live your life, which is the heart of biblical modesty and honors the God we profess to worship.

Epilogue

When I first decided to write a topical sermon on modesty in college, I had no idea where it would lead me. I had no idea the hours of research I would do and all the things I would learn. I had no idea that it would lead to two Bible studies, a spoken word poem on YouTube, and a small video series on YouTube. I had no idea that all this research and all these projects would turn into a passion. I had no idea how embracing these truths would change the way I see myself, as well as the way I saw everyone around me. I definitely had no idea this passion would drive me to self-publish my first book.

As I look back on the last seven years of my life, I know that all the difficult circumstances that I've faced have been easier to bear when I embraced the truth that Jesus died for me so I can live for Him. I am humbled to have the opportunity to share what I have learned about biblical modesty in this book and that you have chosen to take the time to read it. The fact that you are reading this book is proof of what a gracious and loving God I serve.

I hope and pray that the truths revealed to you in this book become real. I hope that you are challenged and inspired to rethink any standards that may not have been founded on God's word. I hope that you have been able to embrace your identity as a daughter (or son) of the King of Kings. I hope that discovering that identity has helped you find freedom within modesty. I hope that you take hold of these truths and stand up for them, even if you face opposition. I hope that you return to this book when you need inspiration. I hope that God spoke through me to a generation that needs to hear this powerful truth:

No matter what anyone has ever said, you are a princess worth dying for.

Appendix 1
The Vanity Fast Challenge

If you struggle with being too concerned with your physical appearance and what others think about you, you're not alone. However, if we want to live a lifestyle of modesty, we have to learn how to take the focus off of ourselves and put it back onto God. Therefore, I want to challenge you to leave your vanity at the foot of the cross by doing a vanity fast.

What is a vanity fast? Fasting is when you give something up for a time to focus more on God. The most common type of fasting, the one that is discussed in the Bible, is abstaining from food. This is because food is something that can quickly become an idol, taking God's place in our hearts. Removing that obstacle will allow you to focus on prayer, but there are plenty of other things that become idols in our hearts, including ourselves. Therefore, a vanity fast is giving up something you depend on related to physical beauty to make sure that God is number one in your heart. If you are still confused about what this means, here are the answers to some questions you may have.

WHAT DO I FAST FROM?

Here are some ideas to get you started:

FASHION FAST
Clothes – give up dressy or trendy clothing. Mostly wear jeans and simple t-shirts
Makeup – don't wear makeup at all
Hair – don't do fancy hairdos, mostly leave it down or doing simple ponytails

Jewelry – give up wearing jewelry, especially "blingy" jewelry

SHOPPING FAST – If you struggle with spending too much money on any of the things listed above, give up buying those things

MIRROR FAST – If you struggle with spending too much time in front of the mirror, then put yourself on a timer. Try to limit yourself to essential mirror time only, like brushing your hair and teeth. If you spend an hour or more in front of the mirror daily, then I recommend limiting yourself to 10 to 15 minutes a day.

MEDIA FAST
Fashion magazines/websites – don't look at articles, websites, or other materials that make you struggle with dwelling on your physical appearance or make you think "I wish I looked like her."
Chick Flicks – don't watch movies or TV shows that make you dwell on your physical appearance or make you think "I wish I looked like her."

SOCIAL MEDIA FAST – If you struggle with concentrating too much on how many likes you get on Instagram or how many retweets you get, then give up going on social media. Delete or restrict the apps on your phone. Try not to take unnecessary selfies or think about who will like your photos when you take them.

ICON FAST – If you struggle with wearing too much of anything that revolves around movies, TV shows, movie stars, music artists, YouTube stars, or something similar, then give up wearing anything of these icons or consuming their products. Consider taking down posters or pictures.

128

For example, I gave up wearing any of my Disney t-shirts and accessories the first time I did this. Try to stick to listening to worship music or watching Christian movies instead.

UGLY FAST – If you struggle with thinking negatively about your appearance, then give up the things that cause you to think you are ugly or fat. Avoid using a scale. Limit your mirror time. Stop comparing yourself to other girls. Ask God to help you see yourself the way He sees you.

OTHER FAST – If you can think of something else that relates to beauty that will challenge you personally, go for it!

HOW DO I CHOOSE WHAT TO FAST FROM?

Pick what you struggle with the most – if you don't struggle with wearing makeup, then don't fast from makeup, because you won't learn anything and it won't bring you closer to God. Pick something that will challenge you.

Ask your parents or other people you trust – they should know you well enough to know your greatest struggles.

Pray – The Lord will reveal to you what He wants you to do if you ask. He knows you better than you know yourself.

WHAT SHOULD I DO DIFFERENTLY WHEN I'M FASTING?

Spend time with the Lord – If you don't have a special time of your day to spend with the Lord, this is a really good time to start. Find a devotional book or pick a book of the Bible to start reading every day. The gospel of Mark would be a good place to start since you can read just a chapter a day for two weeks and mostly finish the book. Pray hard, but also be listening for what the Lord may be telling you.

Don't make a big deal out of it – If you're a teen, you should tell your parents or possibly your siblings. If you're an adult, you should tell a few close friends so they can support and encourage you. Aside from that, don't announce the fact that you are fasting. If someone notices or asks about it you can tell them, but don't make a spectacle out of what you are doing. Jesus said when you fast, you should "anoint your head and wash your face" (Matthew 6:17 NIV). This means that we should still be taking care of our basic needs so we are not drawing unnecessary attention to ourselves.

Honor any wardrobe rules – If you are doing anything from the fashion fast, remember to honor your parents' rules about when you need to dress up. You should also honor the rules of any given institution, such as school or work. When you honor those rules, you are honoring the Lord.

Pay attention – Notice how different life is when you have given up these things. Pay special attention to when it is difficult to fight the temptation to be vain or dwell on your appearance. Ask the Lord to help you when it gets difficult.

Point people to God – Get up every day asking "What can I do today to point people back to Jesus?"

HOW LONG SHOULD I FAST?

That is between you and the Lord. While most food fasts last a few days, this sort of fast is usually more effective when done over longer periods. I recommend 2 to 6 weeks, but if you feel you need to do it for longer, then do whatever the Lord is calling you to do. Once you set a timeframe, stick to it.

Should I do this with my friends?

Absolutely! If you have one or more friends that want to do this with you, then go for it! Support and encouragement are both important when taking on a challenge like this. Maybe you can do the same book for devotions or do a small Bible study together. There is always strength in numbers, so I encourage you to find friends who will do this with you.

What should I do when I'm done?

When your fast is complete, ask the Lord what you should do next. If you feel the Lord is calling you to give up something permanently, ask the Lord to give you the strength to do it. If you need to figure out how to reintroduce anything you fasted from back into your life, ask the Lord to help you not fall back into the temptation of worldly vanity. If you do this with friends, discuss what you learned together and talk about how you can live a life that isn't vain but rather is humble.

If this experience has gone well for you, I'd love to hear about it. Send me an email at princessworthdyingfor@gmail.com.

[Note: Credit goes to Dannah Gresh for suggesting the vanity fast idea in *The Secret Keeper Devotional*.[1]]

Appendix 2
A Note to Men on Modesty

Guys, many of you dress immodestly too. Some of you may be surprised to hear me say that, but it's true. Just like self-esteem and body image issues, modesty isn't just a female problem, but our culture treats it like it is. While it seems that many traditional modesty standards for women have gone out the window, men have often been left completely off the hook. From men who are not afraid to show off their muscles to guys who wear their pants down to their knees, immodest men are everywhere. It's to the point that even young girls are noticing this double standard.

If you're reading this, it's probably because your daughter, wife, mom, or another woman passed it along to you. Since you may only read this section, I will retell a story I shared earlier. The first time I ever taught a Bible study, I invited the dads of the girls to join us one night so the girls could hear a man's/father's perspective on modesty. After I asked the dads a few questions, I opened up the floor for the girls to ask anything they wanted. They were feeling pretty shy about it. They were kind of huddled together, trying to figure out what they were going to ask. When I came over to them, I managed to figure out the one question they were hesitant to ask: why do girls have to dress modestly, but guys don't? I was surprised that these young girls came up with such a profound question. Frankly, so were their dads. It made a point that has stuck with me ever since. I hope it does with you too.

HUMILITY AND MODESTY

Just because the passages about modesty in Scripture are addressed to women doesn't mean that the concepts don't also apply to you. Modesty is having humility in the way you present yourself so that you can point people to God. The call to humble ourselves before the Lord is one that God gives to all of us, male or female. It's at the very heart of what Jesus did for us on the cross. Just like Paul tells us in Philippians:

"Do nothing from selfish ambition or conceit, but in humility count others more significant than yourselves. Let each of you look not only to his own interests, but also to the interests of others. Have this mind among yourselves, which is yours in Christ Jesus, who, though he was in the form of God, did not count equality with God a thing to be grasped, but emptied himself, by taking the form of a servant, being born in the likeness of men. And being found in human form, he humbled himself by becoming obedient to the point of death, even death on a cross. Therefore God has highly exalted him and bestowed on him the name that is above every name, so that at the name of Jesus every knee should bow, in heaven and on earth and under the earth, and every tongue confess that Jesus Christ is Lord, to the glory of God the Father." (Philippians 2:3-11 ESV)

This mindset of humility should be shared by the body of Christ as a whole, not just women. As you consider how you might humble yourself in your physical presentation, I will give you a few tips from a female perspective. This is not meant to demean you or to exercise authority over you. This is a sister in Christ offering some advice about what would be helpful to us.

TIPS FOR MALE MODESTY

<u>Don't Flaunt Your Body or Your Muscles</u> – Although I think that staying physically fit is a good thing, some men take it over the top with bodybuilding. There are several jobs and situations where having muscles and upper body strength is important, but if the main reason for doing it is to make your body more attractive, then you're not coming at it from the right place. If you do choose to body build, don't make your body or muscles the center of attention. Don't wear tight shirts and don't be showing off your strength to impress the girls. Speaking of tight clothes, skinny jeans on most men draw a lot of attention to the lower half of your body and I encourage you to be cautious about wearing them. Avoid walking around shirtless outside of appropriate activities like swimming. Mowing the lawn and playing sports are not the right places to be going around shirtless. It can become a real hindrance to many women who desire to pursue purity.

<u>Get a Belt</u> – Just like I told the girls earlier in this book, "plumber's crack" and exposing your underwear is one way to guarantee attention being drawn to yourself. It doesn't help your witness for Christ or your sisters in Christ. I can tell you from a girl's perspective, it makes us pretty uncomfortable to see it. However, there is usually a simple solution to this problem: get a belt. If you don't already, you should wear a belt with all the pants that have belt loops, including your jeans. This helps make sure that your pants stay around your waist. Problem solved! (You may also want to check that your pants are the right size. If your pants are too big, they will continue to fall down on you, even with a belt).

Tuck Your Undershirt Into Your Pants – As I told the girls earlier in the book, I am so thankful that they don't make belly shirts and crop tops for guys! The longer lengths of your undershirts and tanks (aka wife beaters) give you an advantage. They are so effective, I encourage the girls to get them! If you have them and wear them, another simple solution to your pants problems is to tuck in your undershirt.

Avoid Speedos – I'm just going to leave this one here. Just don't go there, please!

Keep it Secret, Keep it Safe – I shared a story earlier about my teacher telling us to remember what Gandalf said to Frodo about the Ring of Power – "Keep it Secret, Keep it Safe." I encourage the girls to remember that one of the goals of modesty is to save the deepest secrets of their beauty for just one man – their husband.[1] As a sister in Christ, I encourage you to learn what it means to save the deepest secret of your manhood for just one woman – your wife.

Dads, Speak Up!

I want to give a word of encouragement to any dads of daughters who are reading this. If you see that your daughter is struggling with modesty, it's your responsibility to speak up. Although your wife shares this responsibility with you, I believe your role in this process is even more important. It's your responsibility to guard and protect her purity until her wedding day. Your role goes beyond correcting her if her outfit is inappropriate. It involves you going out of your way to affirm her value as your daughter, as a creation of the God of the universe, and as a young woman that Christ died to redeem. Affirming your love and Christ's love for her is a part of your job as her father.

I want to share with you a story about a father who was willing to speak up about his daughter's modesty and her worth: boxing champion Muhammad Ali. One day, while visiting with his daughters, he noticed that one of them was wearing revealing clothing, and he told her:

"Hana, everything that God made valuable in the world is covered and hard to get to. Where do you find diamonds? Deep down in the ground, covered and protected. Where do you find pearls? Deep down at the bottom of the ocean, covered up and protected in a beautiful shell. Where do you find gold? Way down in the mine, covered over with layers and layers of rock. You've got to work hard to get to them...Your body is sacred. You're far more precious than diamonds and pearls, and you should be covered too."[2]

I hope that this story inspires you to have a similar conversation with your daughter(s) because this is something that every girl or young woman needs to hear. Before you correct her immodesty, you need to make sure that she knows how much you love her and how much Jesus loves her. I pray that none of you take this responsibility lightly. Then you can build a rapport with her so that she seeks your approval for things like her prom dress and someday her wedding dress. That's the kind of relationship I still have with my dad. I hope you can build that with your daughter too.

DON'T BE AFRAID TO ASK

I feel that this is only scratching the surface of the topics of male modesty and a father's involvement in his daughter's modesty journey. I wish we could get male leaders in the church to start talking about male modesty. I hope that this discussion has at least opened your eyes to the importance of presenting ourselves in a way that honors the God we worship. If you want to gain more perspective on what you should keep covered, ask your wife or mom. Start some discussions with leaders in your church or other men you trust about what male modesty looks like. Don't be afraid to ask the questions that will help you live a life that will better honor the Lord and your Christian sisters. I believe that if both men and women in the church learn how to embrace modesty and humility, this world would never be the same.

Video and Article Links

Throughout this book, I make references to videos and articles that have been incredibly helpful to me on my journey to understanding biblical modesty. To make these resources easier to access, I am sharing a collection of QR codes and hyperlinks to help you access them. Most of these videos and articles are also cited in the notes.

Introduction – How Frozen Should Have Ended – Reissued (by How It Should Have Ended)

https://youtu.be/Dach1nPbsY8

Chapter 3 – Stephanie Giese's 1st Post – "A Target Intervention on Behalf of Our Daughters"

binkiesandbriefcases.com/target-intervention-behalf-daughters/

Stephanie Giese's 2ⁿᵈ Post – "Dressing Our Daughter: How Target Responded to My Last Post"

http://binkiesandbriefcases.com/dessing-our-daughters/

Chapter 4 – David Platt 1 Timothy 2 Sermon (Note: the section about verses 9-10 starts at 15:28 and lasts about 7 minutes)

https://radical.net/sermon/what-about-women-paul

Chapter 5 – "Who You Are: A Message to All Women" (By Jon Jorgenson)

https://youtu.be/uWi5iXnguTU

Chapter 6 – YouTube Playlist For Mediation of Jesus on the Cross

https://www.youtube.com/playlist?list=PLCf7yxT6HvCcFd
cluKkskDY5Y18C-QMsK

Chapter 11 – The Evolution of the Swimsuit by Jessica Rey

https://youtu.be/WJVHRJbgLz8

Chapter 12 – Two Women Arrested in Chicago for Wearing One-Piece Suits in 1922

https://rarehistoricalphotos.com/women-arrested-bathing-suits-1920s

Videos from My YouTube Channel about Modesty

Beyond Your Wardrobe || Spoken Word

https://youtu.be/hasuLyS_wkI

Princess Worth Dying For || Spoken Word

https://www.youtube.com/watch?v=zQSVBgutADM

Mission Modesty Series Playlist (Includes Original Modesty Sermon and 3 episodes of a show called Mission Modesty)

https://www.youtube.com/playlist?list=PLCf7yxT6HvCe4u o6u2KCJJ7jVhZJoXDeH

Recommended Readings

Books about Modesty/Purity (For Pre-Teen Girls)

True Girl: Discover the Secrets of True Beauty by Dannah Gresh*
True Girl: Mom Daughter Devos by Dannah Gresh**
Lies Girls Believe by Dannah Gresh

Books about Modesty (For Teens/Young Adult Women)

Secret Keeper: The Delicate Power of Modesty by Dannah Gresh
Secret Keeper Devotional by Dannah Gresh
Decent Exposure by Jessica Rey and Leah Darrow
Project Modesty (E-Book) by Kristen Clark and Bethany Baird
The Look: Does God Really Care About What I Wear by Nancy DeMoss Wolgemuth

Books about Purity (For Teens/Young Adult Women)

Sex, Purity, and the Longings of a Girl's Heart by Kristen Clark and Bethany Beal
What Are You Waiting For by Dannah Gresh
Every Young Woman's Battle by Shannon Ethridge and Stephen Arterburn
21 Myths (Even Good) Girls Believe about Sex by Jennifer Strickland
Lies Young Women Believe by Nancy DeMoss Wolgemuth and Dannah Gresh
And the Bride Wore White: The Seven Secrets to Sexual Purity by Dannah Gresh

Books about Self-Worth/Identity

Spoken For: Embracing Who You Are and Whose You Are by Robin Jones Gunn and Alyssa Joy Bethke

Girl Defined: God's Radical Design for Beauty, Femininity, and Identity by Kristen Clark and Bethany Baird
Lies Young Women Believe by Nancy DeMoss Wolgemuth and Dannah Gresh
Got Lost: Your Guide to Finding True Love by Dannah Gresh
Radiant by Priscilla Shirer

Books about Strengthening Your Virtues (For Teens/Young Adult Women)

Choosing Forgiveness by Nancy Leigh DeMoss
Choosing Gratitude by Nancy Leigh DeMoss

*Previously published under the title *Secret Keeper Girl: The Power of Modesty for Tweens*

**Previously published under the title *Secret Keeper Girl: Mom Daughter Devos*

Notes

Intro

[1] Baxter, Daniel and Tina Anderson. "How Frozen Should Have Ended – Reissued." *YouTube*, 4 June 2014, youtu.be/Dach1nPbsY8.

Chapter 1

[1] Wolgemuth, Nancy DeMoss. *Lies Women Believe*. Chicago, IL: Moody Publishers, 2018, 78.

[2] Gresh, Dannah. *Lies Girls Believe*. Chicago, IL: Moody Publishers, 2019, 66.

[3] Wolgemuth, Nancy DeMoss and Dannah Gresh. *Lies Young Women Believe*. Chicago, IL: Moody Publishers, 2018, 72.

[4] Gresh, Dannah. *The Secret Keeper: The Delicate Power of Modesty*. Chicago, IL: Moody Publishers, 2011, 60.

[5] Clark, Kristen and Bethany Baird. *Girl Defined: God's Radical Design for Beauty, Femininity, and Identity.* Grand Rapids, MI: Baker Books, 2016, 58.

[6] "Jessica Rey - The Evolution of the Swimsuit." *YouTube*, 17 June 2013, youtu.be/WJVHRJbgLz8.

Chapter 2

[1] Gresh, Dannah. "Secret Keeper [DVD]" Chicago, IL: Moody Publishers, 2005.

Chapter 3

[1] Giese, Stephanie. "A Target Intervention on Behalf of My Daughters." *Binkies and Briefcases*, 20 September 2014,

binkiesandbriefcases.com/target-intervention-behalf-daughters/

[2] Giese, Stephanie. "Dressing Our Daughters: How Target Responded to My Last Post." *Binkies and Briefcases*, 17 April 2015, binkiesandbriefcases.com/dessing-our-daughters/.

Chapter 4

[1] Tolkien, J.R.R. *The Lord of the Rings: The Fellowship of the Ring*. New York, NY: Houghton Mifflin Co., 1954, 36.

[2] Gresh, Dannah. "Secret Keeper [DVD]" Chicago, IL: Moody Publishers, 2005.

[3] Platt, David. "What About Women, Paul?" *Radical.net*, 21 Aug. 2018, radical.net/sermon/what-about-women-paul/.

Chapter 5

[1] Jorgenson, Jon. "Who You Are: A Message to All Women." *YouTube*, 18 July 2013, youtu.be/uWi5iXnguTU

Chapter 6

[1] Strobel, Lee. *The Case for Christ*. Grand Rapids, MI: Zondervan, 2016, Ch 11.

[2] Nicole Nordeman. *Why*, Grant Cummingham, London, England, 23 May 2000.

[3] Casting Crowns. *Who Am I*, Mark A. Miller, Franklin, TN, 22 February 2004.

[4] MIKESCHAIR. *Someone Worth Dying For*, Matt Bronleewe, 23 August 2011.

[5] Moore, Mark. *The Chronological Life of Christ*. Joplin, MO: College Press, 2007, 642.

Chapter 9

[1] "Breastfeeding in Public." *Wikipedia*, Wikimedia Foundation, 6 Feb. 2020, en.wikipedia.org/wiki/Breastfeeding_in_public.

Chapter 11

[1] "Jessica Rey - The Evolution of the Swimsuit." *YouTube*, 17 June 2013, youtu.be/WJVHRJbgLz8.

[2] Clark, Kristen and Bethany Baird. *Project Modesty: How to Honor God with Your Wardrobe While Looking Totally Adorable in the Process* [Ebook]. San Antonio, TX: Girl Defined Ministries, 2015, Ch. 12.

Chapter 12

[1] "Bathing Machine." *Wikipedia*, Wikimedia Foundation, 3 Jan. 2020, en.wikipedia.org/wiki/Bathing_machine.

[2] Leo, and CARL Zimbiri. "Women Being Arrested for Wearing One Piece Bathing Suits, 1920s." *Rare Historical Photos*, 29 Oct. 2016, rarehistoricalphotos.com/women-arrested-bathing-suits-1920s/.

Appendix 1

[1] Gresh, Dannah. *The Secret Keeper Devotional*. Chicago, IL: Moody Publishers, 2011, 85-87.

Appendix 2

[1] Gresh, Dannah. "Secret Keeper [DVD]" Chicago, IL: Moody Publishers, 2005.

[2] Ali, Hana. *More than a Hero: Muhammad Ali's Life Lessons Presented Through His Daughter's Eyes*. London, England: Coronet, 2001.

BETHEL GROVE is a book blogger, YouTuber, spoken word artist, and a graduate of Ozark Christian College. She loves to use her platforms to proclaim the truth of the gospel and to promote others who do the same. To those that know her, she's simply a woman who is young at heart that loves Reese's Peanut Butter Cups, Disney Princess movies, and the color red.

If you enjoy this book, make sure to check out Bethel's other resources online:

WWW.PRINCESSWORTHDYINGFOR.COM

 Princess Worth Dying For Ministries

 @PrincessWD4

 @princessworthdyingfor

 Princess Worth Dying For

 princessworthdyingfor@gmail.com

WERE YOU INSPIRED OR ENCOURAGED BY THIS BOOK? THEN SHARE ABOUT IT WITH OTHERS!

- Share about the book on social media. Use the hashtags #beyondyourwardrobebook and #princessworthdyingfor

- Write a review on your blog or retail sites

- Purchase copies for family or friends, especially those that you feel need to hear its message

- Recommend this book to your church, book club, class, or local library

- Ask your favorite book store if they carry it. Even if they don't currently have it, it will increase the likelihood that they start to carry it if enough people ask

Made in United States
Orlando, FL
14 May 2022

17849602R00093